Pathfinder®Guides

CW01391847

South Devon and Dartmoor

Walks

*Fully revised by
Sue Viccars*

Contents

At-a-glance

Walk		Page					
1	Cockington Valley	10	Cockington	SX 894638	2¾ miles (4.4km)	445ft (135m)	1½ hrs
2	Bench Tor	12	Venford Reservoir	SX 685712	2½ miles (4km)	425ft (130m)	1½ hrs
3	Gara Rock and Portlemouth Down	14	Mill Bay, East Portlemouth	SX 741380	3½ miles (5.6km)	375ft (115m)	2 hrs
4	Stover Country Park and the River Teign	16	Stover Country Park	SX 832749	5 miles (7.8km)	130ft (40m)	2 hrs
5	Vixen Tor and Pew Tor	18	¾ mile west of Merrivale Bridge	SX 540749	4 miles (6.5km)	525ft (160m)	2 hrs
6	Exe Estuary and Exminster Marshes	20	Powderham church	SX 972844	5½ miles (8.7km)	n/a	2½ hrs
7	The Yealm Estuary	22	Noss Mayo	SX 547474	4½ miles (7.2km)	460ft (140m)	2½ hrs
8	Venn Ottery Common	24	Tipton St John	SY 090917	5 miles (7.9km)	490ft (150m)	2½ hrs
9	Dart Estuary and Dartmouth Castle	26	Little Dartmouth	SX 874491	3¾ miles (5.9km)	720ft (220m)	2½ hrs
10	Broadhembury	28	Broadhembury	ST 101047	4½ miles (7.2km)	590ft (180m)	2½ hrs
11	Loddiswell and the Avon Valley Woods	32	Loddiswell	SX 720485	5¼ miles (8.3km)	425ft (130m)	3 hrs
12	Ashburton and Whiddon Scrubbs	35	Ashburton Town Hall	SX 755699	5½ miles (8.8km)	655ft (200m)	3 hrs
13	Three Reservoirs Walk	38	Trenchford Reservoir	SX 804823	5¾ miles (9.1km)	460ft (140m)	3 hrs
14	Brixham and Churston Point	41	Brixham Harbour	SX 925562	6 miles (9.5km)	525ft (160m)	3 hrs
15	Prawle Point and Woodcombe Point	44	Prawle Point	SX 774354	5¾ miles (9.1km)	690ft (210m)	3 hrs
16	Otter Estuary, East Budleigh and Otterton	47	Budleigh Salterton	SY 072820	6¾ miles (10.6km)	150ft (45m)	3 hrs
17	Kingston and the River Erme	50	Kingston	SX 635478	5¾ miles (9.1km)	1,035ft (315m)	3 hrs
18	Bolt Head and Salcombe Estuary	54	North Sands, Salcombe	SX 730382	6 miles (9.4km)	920ft (280m)	3½ hrs
19	Start Point and Hallsands	57	Start Point	SX 820375	6½ miles (10.4km)	935ft (285m)	3½ hrs
20	Torcross, Slapton Ley and Stokenham	60	Torcross	SX 823424	7 miles (11.2km)	755ft (230m)	3½ hrs
21	Beer and Branscombe	63	Beer, Cliff Top car park	SY 228888	6¼ miles (9.9km)	1,180ft (360m)	3½ hrs
22	Rippon Tor, Pil Tor and Buckland Beacon	66	Cold East Cross	SX 740742	6½ miles (10.3km)	1,035ft (315m)	3½ hrs
23	Widgery Cross and Great Links Tor	69	NE of Dartmoor Inn, off A386 nr Lydford	SX 525853	6½ miles (10.5km)	1,130ft (345m)	3½ hrs
24	Yes Tor and High Willhays	72	Okehampton Moor Gate	SX 591931	6¼ miles (9.9km)	1,015ft (310m)	3½ hrs
25	Sidmouth, Salcombe Regis and Weston Combe	76	Sidmouth	SY 125871	8 miles (12.8km)	1,345ft (410m)	4 hrs
26	Princetown, Dartmoor Railway and Leather Tor	80	Princetown	SX 589735	10 miles (15.8km)	985ft (300m)	5 hrs
27	Dittisham, Cornworthy and Tuckenhay	84	Dittisham	SX 864550	9½ miles (15.2km)	1,790ft (545m)	5½ hrs
28	Buckfastleigh Moor	88	Holne	SX 706694	10 miles (15.8km)	1,855ft (565m)	6 hrs

Comments

A short walk from an idyllic village and through a lovely secluded valley, all within a short distance of the seafront at Torquay.

On this walk you get one of the finest views over Dartmoor for very little effort.

A gentle ascent along a beautiful wooded track is followed by a splendid coastal walk with fine views across the Salcombe Estuary.

A circuit of a lake, plus woodland, meadow and riverside walking, following an easy and well-waymarked trail.

Boggy conditions can be expected at times on this fine scenic walk across open moorland that takes in several tors.

A fresh, open walk across marshes and by a canal and river estuary, but after rain some muddy stretches can be expected.

There could hardly be a flatter or easier coastal walk in South Devon as it follows a carriage drive laid out by a local Victorian landowner.

This walk climbs out of the valley on to one of the remaining expanses of open heathland in south east Devon.

Expect quite a lot of climbing on this short walk that takes in a late medieval castle and offers spectacular views across the estuary.

From a picturesque thatched village with a fine medieval church follow the route round the edge of a typical, well-wooded Devonian combe.

A delightful and relaxing ramble through steep sided riverside woodlands which is the highlight of this walk.

After walking through a thickly wooded valley, the final part of the route offers fine views over the southern fringes of Dartmoor.

Three reservoirs on the eastern fringes of Dartmoor are linked by this walk, much of which is through conifer woodland.

The walk takes you along the stretch of coast to the west of the fishing town of Brixham, on the fringes of Torbay.

Pass the most southerly point on the South Devon coast on a walk which runs along one of its most spectacular stretches.

The route starts at a small seaside resort by the estuary and explores a delightfully scenic river valley, taking in two attractive villages and passing a restored mill.

A magical exploration of one of South Devon's least visited corners – enjoy the tranquil estuary of the River Erme and a rugged stretch of coastal walking with some steep descents.

A rugged but easy section of coastline is followed at the end by a dramatic walk along the western side of the estuary.

From the headland at the start, the views encompass a long stretch of coast from Torbay to the Salcombe Estuary.

Memories of a Second World War disaster, a nature reserve based around a lagoon, and a splendid medieval church provide plenty of interest and variety.

An energetic and highly scenic route that includes two attractive villages , a Norman church, fine coastal woodlands and some superb cliff walking.

Five tors are climbed on this walk, all of them with magnificent viewpoints and there is also the opportunity to take in an idyllic, tucked away thatched hamlet.

The whole of this walk, which involves one steep climb, is across open moorland and the views, especially over West Devon are amazing.

This walk to the two highest points in southern England offers the most superb and extensive views.

There are a number of stiff climbs, especially along the switchback cliffs on the final part of the walk, but the outstanding views more than compensate.

A lengthy but not strenuous walk which offers the experience of Dartmoor at its wildest and bleakest.

A wonderfully winding route with some steep climbs and muddy and overgrown paths in places, but varied and absorbing also, with some superb views.

Much of this challenging walk is across pathless moorland and the route is best left for fine weather when the extensive views can be appreciated to the full.

Keymap

10 Broadhembury

Honiton

Crediton

Okehampton

Exe

Roadford Lake (reservoir)

24

D E V O N

Exeter

Tipton St John

8

Seato

Lydford

23

Moretonhampstead

Teign

Exminster

Topsham

Sidmouth

25

21 Beer

6

13

16

Fernworthy Reservoir

Lustleigh

Exmouth

Budleigh Salterton

Dartmoor

Merrivale

Buckland in the Moor

22

4 Teigngrace

Dawlish

Lyme Bay

Tavistock

5

26 Princetown

2 Holne

12 Ashburton

Teignmouth

Tamar

28

Newton Abbot

Tavy

Burrator Reservoir

Buckfastleigh

1 Cockington

Torquay

Plym

altash

Dart

Totnes

Paignton

Tor Bay

Plymouth

Ivybridge

27 Dittisham

Brixham

14 Berry Head

Dartmouth

9

Noss Mayo

Loddiswell

7

17 Kingston

11

Rame Head

Stokenham

20 Start Bay

Bigbury Bay

Salcombe

18 **3** **15** **19** Start Point

Bolt Head

Prawle Point

The tank memorial at Torcross

Introduction to South Devon and Dartmoor

This South Devon guide adds to the choice of excellent walks available in Pathfinder Guide Dartmoor. Beyond the National Park it explores the glorious South Devon countryside more widely on the hills and in the river valleys of the South Hams and south east Devon, and especially along the spectacular coastline, the jewel of the region – thus increasing the choice and variety.

At the crossroads of South Devon is Exeter, ancient Roman settlement, medieval cathedral city and county town. To the west lies the great granite massif of Dartmoor, while to the south east, south and south west the long line of the coast stretches from Beer near the Dorset border to Plymouth on the fringes of Cornwall. The transition from coast to moor is quite a dramatic and sudden one. A short journey northwards from Torquay – where in the almost subtropical conditions palm trees grow on the promenade – subjects you to one of the most abrupt changes of scenery likely to be encountered anywhere in this country. A few miles in distance and a few hundred feet in height transports you to the last great wilderness in southern England, the open and majestic terrain of Dartmoor, parts of which are as bleak and remote as anywhere in the wildest regions of the northern Pennines.

Vixen Tor

Dartmoor

As well as being justifiably acclaimed as the last great wilderness in southern England, Dartmoor also contains the highest land in England south of the Pennines. Main roads across the moor are relatively few and side roads and country lanes are often narrower than in other parts of the country – as many an exasperated holiday motorist is able to testify. The few towns and villages are mostly concentrated around the edge of the moor, particularly in the river valleys and the gentler country on the south and east, while on the wilder expanses of the north and west they are largely non-existent.

The central heartland of the open moor is surrounded by rolling downs, thickly wooded gorges and pleasant river valleys with picture postcard villages of thatch and granite. The valleys are benign and welcoming but in contrast the moors can be most inhospitable, even dangerous, and as such need to be treated with respect and caution. Route finding across these bare expanses can be difficult as paths tend to peter out, and the lack of easily identifiable landmarks means it is easy for walkers to get lost, especially in misty conditions. But these austere, sweeping moorlands, their hilltops studded with the ubiquitous granite tors – the most characteristic element of the Dartmoor landscape – are endowed with a haunting and melancholic beauty that is undeniably appealing.

From the largely uninhabited central wilderness rise Dartmoor's rivers – the Lyd, Tavy, Meavy, Walkham, Plym, Yealm, Erme, Avon, East and West Dart, Bovey, Teign, Taw and Okement – all of which, except the last two, flow southwards to the English Channel. The reasons for the flow of the rivers and for the wilder scenery being in the north and west lie in the geology and climate of the region. Dartmoor is a great mass of granite rising above the surrounding farmlands like a brooding giant. Immense primeval earth movements tilted this mass towards the south and east, which explains why the highest (and wettest) land is in the north and west and why the majority of the rivers flow southwards. The granite core is edged with areas of softer rocks – slates, shales, limestone and sandstone – and where the rivers leave the harder granite and reach these softer rocks, they have sometimes cut deep narrow ravines, such as the gorges of the Dart, Teign and Lyd.

The tors are remnants of hard masses of granite, moulded into their present shapes by millions of years of weathering. The most conspicuous of these – Haytor Rocks, Hound Tor, Vixen Tor – are not only impressive in themselves but act as vital landmarks for walkers in an otherwise often featureless landscape. Historical remains from all ages lie scattered over Dartmoor, evidence both of continuous occupation and of the long history of human exploitation of the moor. Few areas of Britain have a higher concentration of prehistoric monuments and these include burial chambers, avenues, standing stones, hut circles and hill forts. The discovery of tin around the middle of the 12th century led to the growth of a flourishing tin-mining industry throughout the Middle Ages and Tudor period, and its relics provide a fertile field for those interested in industrial archaeology.

Later in the 19th century there was a great demand for Dartmoor granite and quarrying boomed. First tramways and later railways were constructed across the moor to transport the granite down to the coast and many of these now disused tracks make excellent, clearly defined walking routes. Demand for water from Plymouth and the fast-growing holiday resorts of Torbay led to the construction of reservoirs on the moor. Since the 1870s the army has used a large part of northern Dartmoor for military training purposes. During the 20th century a number of conifer plantations were established. All these developments have left their mark on the present-day landscape of Dartmoor and, like the disused railway tracks and earlier routeways, water board and forestry tracks and army roads – which some purists decry – can be used by walkers to aid navigation and provide relatively easy, well-surfaced routes.

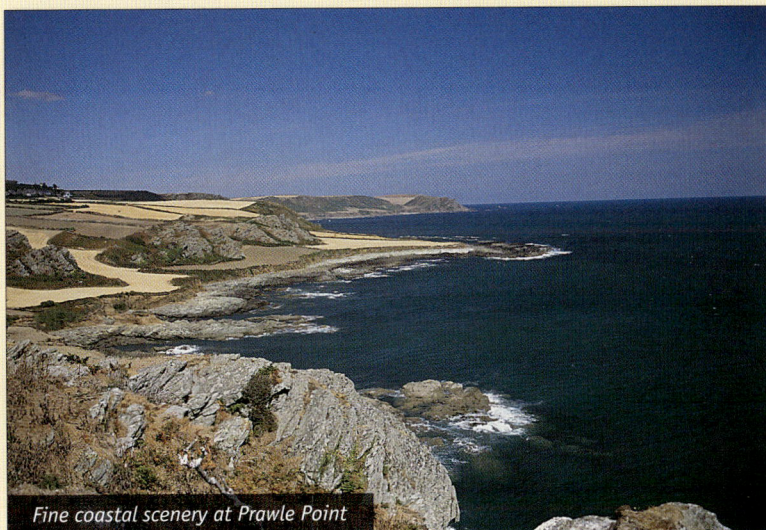
Fine coastal scenery at Prawle Point

The long history of mineral working on Dartmoor is over and the mainstay of the economy nowadays, as with the rest of South Devon, is tourism. As a recognition of its immense landscape value and recreational role, Dartmoor was designated one of Britain's first national parks in 1951.

South Devon

Spreading out like a fan to the south and south east of Dartmoor is a landscape that is typically Devonian, a region of soft, rolling, well-wooded hills, lush pastures and deep river valleys leading on to long, winding estuaries and the coast. The area immediately to the south, bounded by the Tamar in the west and Dart in the east and forming a triangular-shaped wedge jutting out into the Channel, is the South Hams. This is rich farming country dotted with attractive villages, imposing medieval churches and fine old towns such as Totnes, Dartmouth and Kingsbridge. The chief glory of the South Hams is its coastline, broken up by the rias or long, deep estuaries

of the Tamar, the various inlets of the Salcombe estuary, Avon, Erme and Dart. These sheltered estuaries provided good harbours and during the Middle Ages Plymouth and Dartmouth developed into major ports and naval bases, a role that the former, the largest city in Devon, has maintained. During the Second World War many of the quiet estuaries and now small ports, fishing villages and genteel resorts along this coast had a new lease of life as they played a vital role in the build-up to the D-Day landings, providing a base for thousands of American forces.

East of the Dart lies Torbay and the start of the popular holiday coast that reaches to the Dorset border. It was during the Napoleonic Wars, when the English aristocracy were cut off from their usual continental haunts, that this area first became popular and many of the resorts – Torquay, Teignmouth, Exmouth and Sidmouth – still retain some of their graceful Regency architecture. The coming of the railways considerably added to the number of visitors, attracted by the combination of a mild and sunny climate, good sandy beaches and outstanding scenery. Nowadays it is still one of the most popular holiday destinations in Britain, made even more accessible by the M5 motorway.

From Torbay eastwards across the Teign and Exe estuaries to Sidmouth and beyond there are some impressive stretches of dark red sandstone cliffs that provide excellent and challenging walking. At Beer Head the red sandstone gives way to gleaming white chalk, heralding the start of the Dorset coast. Inland there is pleasant countryside in the two main river valleys of the Otter and Sid, with more attractive villages of thatched cottages and imposing churches and some surviving areas of rough heathland standing above the neat and orderly farmland. In 2001 the 95 mile (155km) stretch of coastline from Exmouth in Devon to Old Harry Rocks in Dorset was designated 'the Jurassic Coast', England's first World Heritage Site, on account of its fantastic geological history.

Walking in the Area
For most walkers the primary attractions in South Devon and Dartmoor are the coast and moor, and the majority of the walks which we feature in this book concentrate on those two areas. In addition, the good walking country in the hills and valleys of the South Hams and south east Devon that lie between has not been ignored. Rights of way throughout the area are generally well-waymarked, except on the central heartland of Dartmoor where they are not always visible on the ground. Here you'll find that routes either strike out across the open moor or capitalise on the many disused, former mining and quarrying tracks. The whole length of the coastline is traversed by the South West Coast Path national trail and presents no real route-finding difficulties, but some of the lesser used paths in the lush country between the coast and moor may well become overgrown during the summer months.

With a choice of open moorland, an often dramatic coastline, wooded river valleys, estuaries and creeks, plus picturesque thatched villages with pubs and tea shops dispensing the traditional local delicacies of pasties, cider and cream teas, the walker in South Devon really is in a position to enjoy the best of all worlds.

This book includes a list of waypoints alongside the description of the walk, so that you can enjoy the full benefits of gps should you wish to. For more information on using your gps, read the Pathfinder® Guide *GPS for Walkers*, by gps teacher and navigation trainer, Clive Thomas (ISBN 978-0-7117-4445-5). For essential information on map reading and basic navigation, read the Pathfinder® Guide *Map Reading Skills* by outdoor writer, Terry Marsh (ISBN 978-0-7117-4978-8). Both titles are available in bookshops or can be ordered online at www.totalwalking.co.uk

The River Otter and disused railway bridge near Tipton St John

walk 1

Start
Cockington

Distance
2¾ miles (4.4km)

Height gain
445 feet (135m)

Approximate time
1½ hours

Route terrain
Easy paths and woodland tracks

P Parking
Cockington village car park (pay & display), signed off A380 ring road, Torquay

Dog friendly
Under control in country park

OS maps
Landranger 202 (Torbay & South Dartmoor), Explorers OL20 (South Devon) or 110 (Torquay & Dawlish)

GPS waypoints
- SX 894 638
- (A) SX 886 639
- (B) SX 888 636
- (C) SX 890 638
- (D) SX 893 637
- (E) SX 889 634
- (F) SX 896 635

Cockington Valley

Despite being almost engulfed by the suburban expansion of Torbay, the secluded and well-wooded Cockington valley has survived untouched as a little enclave of traditional, rural England complete with thatched village, meadows, woods and parkland. It has been designated as a country park (gates locked at dusk) and this short walk explores the many facets of this unusual, fascinating and picturesque valley.

Cockington

Thatched and colour-washed cottages, forge, mill with water wheel, pub, cricket field, church and manor house, all tucked away in a tranquil and wooded valley, make Cockington the archetypal English village of calendars and picture postcards. Its proximity to Torquay – only 1 mile from the seafront – makes it inevitably popular with holidaymakers, and the amenities that it offers to visitors – gift shops, Devon cream teas and horse-drawn open carriage rides around the village – only add to the quaintness of the scene. The church and manor house are a short distance from the village centre and these will be passed later on during the walk.

Begin by turning right out of the visitor centre car park along the lane, passing to the right of **The Drum Inn**. This only dates from the 1930s but was designed by Sir Edwin Lutyens to harmonise with its 'olde-world' surroundings. At a public footpath sign to 'Marldon via Bewhay Lane', turn left along an enclosed, sunken track which heads uphill and emerges into more open country, later becoming a hedge-lined path. Ignore a waymarked track left. At the 'Horse Riding Route' sign, follow the path around in a complete U-turn (A). Go through a gate and turn right to continue, between a fence on the left and hedge on the right, above the head of the valley, with fine views to the left of Cockington Court and the church below, and Torquay and the coast on the skyline beyond.

Keep along this undulating path to where it bends first to the left and then sharply to the right. At this point (B) keep ahead down steps to a public footpath sign for Cockington Court a few yards ahead, and turn left over a stile. Follow the narrow path gently downhill by a fence on the left, entering woodland and winding down to a stile. Climb the stile and a few yards ahead turn right (C) over another stile on to a tarmac path through the grounds of Cockington Court, passing between the house on the left and church on the right, side by side in the traditional English manner.

In front of the house turn right along the broad tarmac drive running through the park beside the cricket field on the left – watch out for horse-drawn

> **Cockington Court** Set amid lovely rolling parkland, the 16th-century manor house now houses craft studios and tearooms. The simple but attractive church, with a low west tower, is of Norman origin. Both buildings are in perfect harmony with their surroundings.

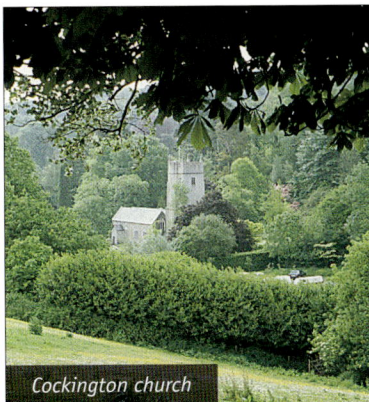

Cockington church

carriages – and, at a fork, take the right-hand track **D**, signposted 'Gamekeeper's Cottage, The Lakes, Seafront'. The track bears to the right, goes through a cutting and under a bridge. At the next fork continue along the right-hand track. Pass to the right of the thatched Gamekeeper's Cottage – burned down in 1990, but since sympathetically restored – and then bear right to continue uphill, signed Warren Barn – now the track will have become rough – along the inside edge of Manscombe Wood.

At a footpath junction in front of Warren Barn turn left **E**, doubling back through the wood. The path passes a green marker post by a fork, and starts to descend. At the next fork look out for where a green marker post directs you to continue along the right-hand, upper path. This is a most attractive stretch of the walk and the earlier track can be seen below. Keep

ahead all the while, passing round two wooden barriers and crossing a path. At a T-junction of paths at the end of the wood turn left and head steeply downhill via a flight of steps to a tarmac path by a small lake. Turn sharp right and then left to rejoin the main tarmac drive. Turn sharp right downhill, passing through a Gothic gatehouse, to a road **F**. Cross over and cross a bridge; turn left along a path, soon rejoining the road and passing **Rose Cottage Tea Gardens** en route to the car park. ●

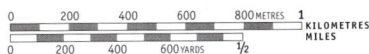

SCALE 1:25 000 or 2½ INCHES to 1 MILE 4CM to 1KM

walk 2

Start

Venford Reservoir

Distance

2½ miles (4km)

Height gain

425 feet (130m)

Approximate time

1½ hours

Route terrain

Moorland and woodland paths

P Parking

Car park (free) on west side of dam, 1½ miles (2.4km) north-west of Holne

Dog friendly

Under control at all times; on leads in nesting season (1 March–15 July)

OS maps

Landranger 202 (Torbay & South Dartmoor), Explorer OL28 (Dartmoor)

GPS waypoints

SX 685 712
Ⓐ SX 687 711
Ⓑ SX 695 713
Ⓒ SX 691 716

Bench Tor

There can be few walks of this modest length that offer such outstanding views and are more enjoyable than this one. From Venford Reservoir you take a clear and easy woodland path that follows the curve of the river above the thickly wooded Dart gorge, eventually climbing steadily to the magnificent viewpoint of Bench Tor. From here it is a gentle descent back to the start.

⚠️ Although a short and easy walk, it is advisable not to attempt it in misty weather as the final section could be difficult without the landmark of the reservoir as a guide.

From the car park head down to the road to cross the dam. On the other side climb a low embankment and then turn left Ⓐ alongside railings which border woodland that surrounds a water treatment works. Where the railings turn left, bear left

A panoramic view over Dartmoor from Bench Tor

and head downhill across grass to join a path which runs just above Venford Brook.

Bear right along this most attractive path – flat, grassy and well constructed. Initially it keeps above the brook but later curves right through steep-sided, rocky woodland, giving excellent views through the trees of the thickly wooded Dart gorge.

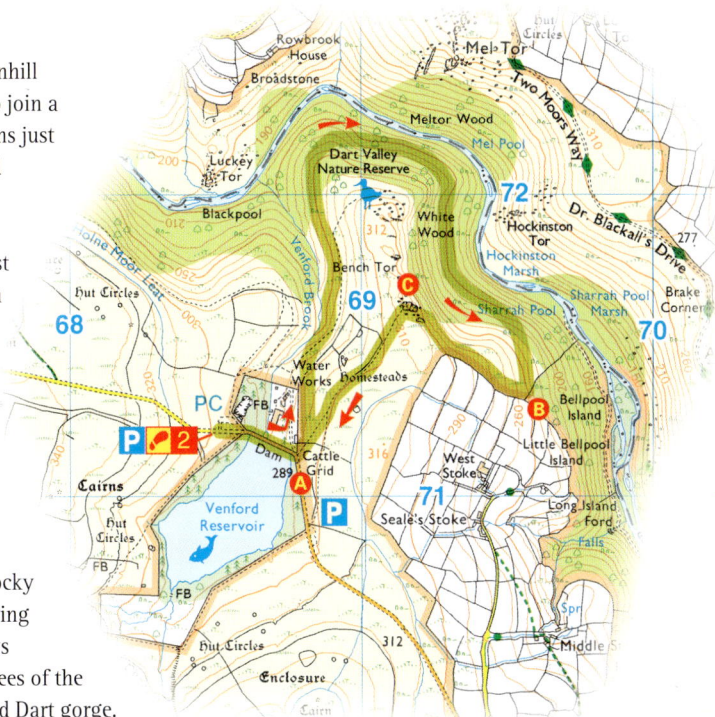

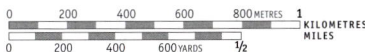

The river is only occasionally glimpsed below but can always be heard. Later the path climbs steadily and emerges from the trees to give another superb view across the Dart valley to the open moor. On reaching a gate, do not go through it but turn right **B** and head uphill, by a wall on the left. Where the wall bears left, keep straight ahead to Bench Tor, bearing right to the highest of the collection of rocks **C** in order to enjoy one of the finest panoramic views over Dartmoor.

Several worn, grassy paths lead from Bench Tor down to the reservoir below; turn left and make your way down, heading for the centre of the reservoir, flanked by conifers. The gentle, almost unnoticeable descent should bring you out on to the road by the end of the dam. Turn right over the dam to return to the starting point. ●

SCALE 1:25 000 or 2½ INCHES to 1 MILE 4CM to 1KM

walk 3

Start
Mill Bay, East Portlemouth

Distance
3½ miles (5.6km)

Height gain
375 feet (115m)

Approximate time
2 hours

Route terrain
Fields and undulating Coast Path

Parking
National Trust car park (pay & display) at Mill Bay, ½ mile (0.8km) south of East Portlemouth (also accessible via passenger ferry from Salcombe)

Dog friendly
On lead in farmland

OS maps
Landranger 202 (Torbay & South Dartmoor), Explorer OL20 (South Devon)

GPS waypoints
SX 741 380
A SX 752 373
B SX 752 370

Gara Rock and Portlemouth Down

From the beach at Mill Bay, a steady uphill climb along a beautiful tree-lined track leads to the coast at the superb viewpoint of Gara Rock. The remainder of the route follows the Coast Path over Portlemouth Down and along the east side of the Salcombe estuary. Towards the end there are particularly fine views across the estuary to Salcombe.

At the beach turn left, at a public bridleway sign for Rickham, along a track that runs beside the car park. For the next ¾ mile follow this most attractive, shady track, lined by old pollarded lime trees, steadily climbing uphill to reach a wooden gate. Go through, cross a track, go up some steps and through a gate to continue uphill along an enclosed, sunken track.

Emerge from the trees, pass through a gate, and walk across the field, passing through a hedge gap. On the far side of the next field go through a gate onto a tarmac track **A**. Turn right along it towards the coast; where it ends follow a low wall to the left, passing the new **Gara Rock** complex (refreshments). On the right here an unusual thatched lookout provides outstanding views along the coast, especially eastwards to Gammon Head. At the fingerpost turn right **B** to join the Coast Path, in the direction of Mill Bay (signposted '2¼ miles').

Pass below the rock, descend steps and follow the winding and undulating coastal path back to the start. At first the view ahead is dominated by Bolt Head. Later the path curves right to continue along the side of the Salcombe estuary, with fine views across to Salcombe itself on the opposite side. Eventually the path passes above beaches, enters woodland and descends to Mill Bay. ●

Map labels:

Whitestrand Quay
39
Ditchend Cove
Ditch End
Horsepool Cove MHW Jetty
The Haven Spr
Ford
PC
Ferry
28
13 Passageway
East Portlemouth
Small's Cove
P
Village Farm
Salcombe
Cumulus
MS
Mill Bay
Ferry P (Summer only)
Salcombe Harbour
MLW
38
134
EAST PORTLEMOU
Holse
Charles
Biddlehead Point
Old Harry Beacon
Sunny Cove
Black Stone
3
P
66
100
129
1·30
120
Spr
High House Farm
Remains of Combe Castle
Pound Stone
Hipples
Battery
74
Rickham Common
South West Coast Path
Portlemouth
81
Rickham
Rickham Cross
114
Spr
76
Catcove Point
Limebury Point
Leek Cove
107
75
A
Down
Spr
The Bar
The Bull
37
B
Gara Rock
Rudder Cove
MLW
09
08
Abraham's Hole
Deckler's Cliff
Deckler's Island

SCALE 1:25 000 or 2½ INCHES to 1 MILE *4CM to 1KM*

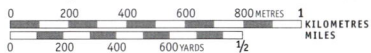

0 200 400 600 800 METRES 1 KILOMETRES
MILES
0 200 400 600 YARDS ½

Looking eastwards from Gara Rock

Start	Stover Country Park
Distance	5 miles (7.8km)
Height gain	130 feet (40m)
Approximate time	2 hours
Route terrain	Level woodland paths, riverside fields, rural lanes
Parking	Stover Country Park (pay & display), ¼ mile (0.4km) south of A38 between Bovey Tracey and Newton Abbot
Dog friendly	On lead in country park
OS maps	Landranger 192 (Okehampton & North Dartmoor), Explorer 110 (Torquay & Dawlish)

GPS waypoints

SX 832 749
Ⓐ SX 836 751
Ⓑ SX 843 749
Ⓒ SX 847 747
Ⓓ SX 854 743
Ⓔ SX 848 741

Stover Country Park and the River Teign

This is an entirely flat walk – a rarity in South Devon. It starts in the wooded surroundings of Stover Country Park, encircles a lake and includes a pleasant stretch of riverside walking beside the Teign. In addition it is an easy walk to follow, well-waymarked with 'Templer Way Heritage Trail' signs.

Stover Country Park

During the 18th century James Templer, a local man, made a fortune from the exploitation of the granite and ball clay resources of Dartmoor, and used some of his wealth to build a grand house surrounded by landscaped parkland in the Teign valley. The house is now a co-ed public school and the grounds form Stover Country Park. The route by which Templer and his successors brought granite down from Haytor and transported ball clay down the Stover Canal to the Teign estuary and the sea is now a waymarked trail, the Templer Way. The Templer Way Heritage Trail is a shorter circular walk that includes the country park, River Teign and Stover Canal.

Start at the information centre and take the track that passes to the left of it into the trees, signed to the Templer Way. Turn right at a T-junction, by a notice board, and the track curves left to the lake which was created by James Templer around 1765 as part of the landscaped grounds of Stover House. Turn left over a footbridge and follow a tree-lined path around Stover Lake. There are attractive views from here across the water, with waterlilies on the surface and rhododendron bushes fringing the edges of the lake. Keep beside the water, curving right all the while and crossing several footbridges. Eventually turn right over a footbridge at the eastern end of the lake to reach a notice board which indicates the start of the Heritage Trail Ⓐ. Turn left, in the direction of the 'Templer Way Heritage Trail via Ventiford', keeping next to a channel on the left.

At the end of the channel, by a cascade, turn right along a path that winds through woodland, later following orange symbols through some rather gloomy conifers, and go through a gate on to the road and turn right. After a few yards turn left Ⓑ, along Summer Lane, and follow it around a right-hand bend and over a railway bridge. At a T-junction turn right; the lane bends right under another railway bridge to rejoin the road. Turn left, soon crossing Ventiford Bridge; immediately turn left Ⓒ along a track, by a brook on the left. Pass under the railway again, keep ahead through a kissing-gate and take the path ahead, which initially keeps along the left edge of a field and later heads across to the River Teign. Go through a kissing-gate and continue along the edge of meadows beside the tree-lined riverbank. Follow the river round a right-hand curve, passing two bridges over the river (cross the second one for refreshments at **Sampson's Farm**). This is a most attractive part of the walk with fine views to the right across the fields to the southern slopes of Dartmoor, with Haytor prominent on the skyline. Look out for a Templer Way post, which directs you to the right **D**, across a meadow, to a kissing-gate. Go through, continue across the meadow, go through another kissing-gate and cross a footbridge over a ditch. Keep ahead to a T-junction of paths, turn right and shortly turn left through a kissing-gate to cross Teigngrace Locks Bridge over the disused Stover Canal, built by the second James Templer to transport ball clay. It ran for 2 miles from Ventiford to the Teign estuary.

Continue over the railway line and along a drive to a road. Turn right and at a Templer Way post, turn left **E** to go through two gates in quick succession – one metal and one wooden. Follow a path across meadows and the tower of Teigngrace church is seen to the left. This too was built by James Templer II, in 1786. Go through a kissing-gate on to a track and turn right, and you will shortly enter woodland. The track emerges from the trees to reach a fork (Stover School left); continue along the right-hand track, between a hedge on the right and woodland on the left, descending into more open country and crossing a bridge.

Pass back into woodland again and just before reaching a footbridge by the Heritage Trail starting point **A**, turn left to complete the circuit of Stover Lake. Cross a footbridge and turn right. At the next footbridge turn left and retrace your steps to the start. ●

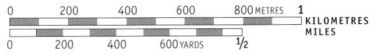

SCALE 1:25 000 or 2½ INCHES to 1 MILE 4CM to 1KM

0	200	400	600	800 METRES	1
					KILOMETRES
					MILES
0	200	400	600 YARDS	½	

Start

¾ mile (1.2km) west of Merrivale Bridge

Distance

4 miles (6.5km)

Height gain

525 feet (160m)

Approximate time

2 hours

Route terrain

Moorland paths and tracks, some rough and wet underfoot

P Parking

Car park (free) on B3357, first on right after Merrivale Quarry, 3½ miles (5.6km) north-west of Princetown

Dog friendly

Under control at all times; on leads in nesting season (1 March–15 July)

OS maps

Landranger 201 (Plymouth & Launceston), Explorer OL28 (Dartmoor)

GPS waypoints

SX 540 749
Ⓐ SX 541 743
Ⓑ SX 535 734
Ⓒ SX 532 734
Ⓓ SX 526 732
Ⓔ SX 526 738
Ⓕ SX 532 742
Ⓖ SX 534 751

Vixen Tor and Pew Tor

The 90ft (28m) Vixen Tor is one of the most distinctive, as well as the tallest, of Dartmoor's tors (known locally as 'the old man in the cap who has turned his back on his wife'!). The walk begins by heading across open moorland to the tor and continues above the western side of the attractive Walkham valley before climbing to the viewpoint of Pew Tor. The route returns across the open expanses of Whitchurch Common, passing the isolated landmark of Windy Post Cross. All the way there are extensive views across moorland to the encircling tors.

Begin by crossing the road and heading straight across the open moor, negotiating boulders, towards the prominent outline of Vixen Tor. Cross a leat, continue – this part is likely to be boggy – and at a wall in front of the tor turn right Ⓐ. Head gently downhill, bending left. Keep near the wall to cross the stream on granite boulders. Continue by the wall on the left, curving right and heading uphill to make your way through an area of gorse, rocks and stunted trees to the left of Heckwood Tor. To the left are fine views over the Walkham valley, ahead the tower of Sampford Spiney church can be seen, and as the path bears right Pew Tor comes into view. Where the wall bends left, keep ahead along the path and, where this curves left shortly afterwards, turn right Ⓑ on to a path that soon bends

The isolated Windy Post Cross – a useful landmark

right and climbs up to Pew Tor **C**, where the magnificent panoramic views include Plymouth Sound.

Continue over the tor, keep on downhill to pass to the left of a disused quarry then follow a grassy path that bears left and heads gently downhill. At the bottom bear left to continue between gorse bushes, alongside a leat on the right. Where the leat runs parallel to a lane, cross the water **D**. Turn sharp right along this narrow lane to where it bends sharp left. Turn right **E** to follow a path gently uphill, keeping parallel to a wall on the left. After the wall turns away left, continue straight ahead across gorse-strewn moorland, fording a leat on a track **F** and bearing slightly

Views from Windy Post Cross

From this ancient landmark, aptly named in view of its exposed and isolated location, there are wide views all around: Vixen Tor, the Walkham valley and King's Tor are to the right and ahead the view is dominated by Cox Tor and Great Staple Tor.

right to follow it to Windy Post Cross.

Continue beside the leat across Whitchurch Common to reach the B3357 **G**. Turn right passing a small car park on the left and return along the road to the starting point. ●

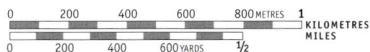

SCALE 1:25 000 or 2½ INCHES to 1 MILE 4CM to 1KM

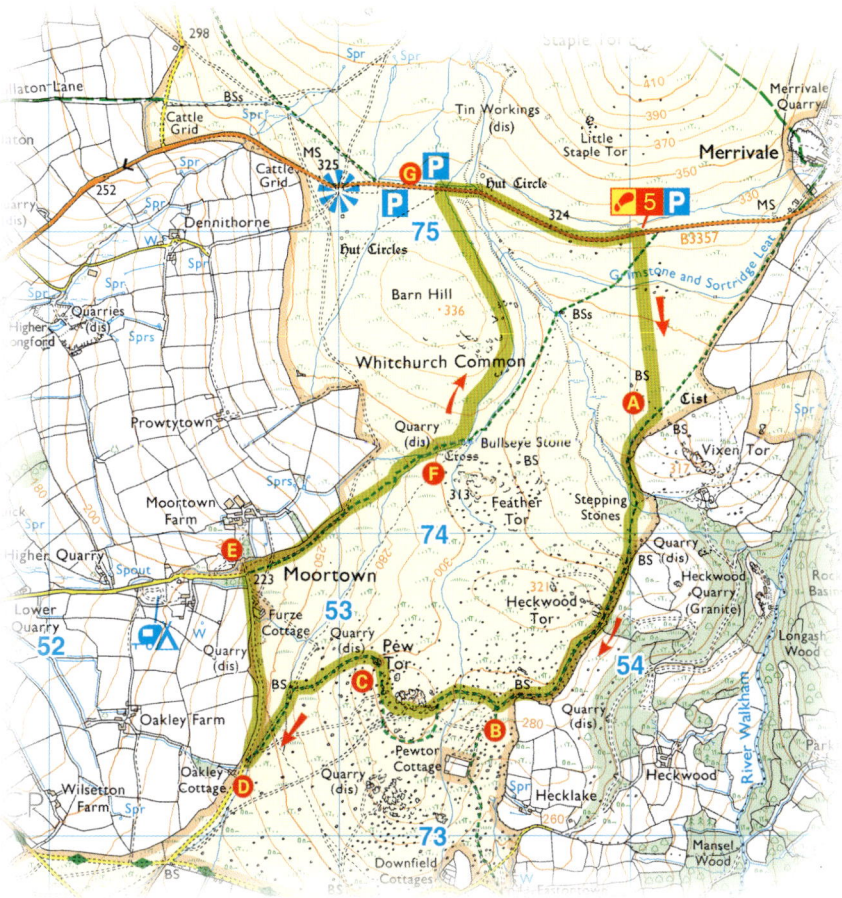

walk 6

Start
Powderham church

Distance
5½ miles (8.7km)

Height gain
Negligible

Approximate time
2½ hours

Route terrain
Level paths, some muddy after wet weather

Parking
Roadside parking spaces by Powderham church (donations)

Dog friendly
On lead in nature reserve

OS maps
Landranger 192 (Exeter & Sidmouth), Explorer 110 (Torquay & Dawlish)

GPS waypoints
🖊 SX 972 844
Ⓐ SX 963 860
Ⓑ SX 954 872
Ⓒ SX 962 879

Exe Estuary and Exminster Marshes

Wide views and fresh, invigorating breezes accompany this flat and easy walk along the west bank of the Exe estuary and across the Exminster Marshes (RSPB reserve), which are a haven for wildlife. The return leg uses the towpath of the Exeter Canal, which runs parallel to the river before emptying into it. Watch out for cyclists on the riverside path: it's a popular route linking Exeter to the South Devon coast.

🖊 Walk down the lane to the left of Powderham church, a fine, red sandstone, mainly 13th-century building. As the lane bends right turn left at a public footpath sign along a track that leads off from the road below a railway embankment on the right. Turn right through a metal kissing-gate to cross the railway line – take care here – and turn left to continue beside the sea wall above the estuary. All around there are wide views: to the right across the Exe, to the left across meadows to low wooded hills, and ahead the buildings of Exeter can be seen in the distance.

The track swings right through a kissing-gate and over a stile to pass to the left of **The Turf** (pub/accommodation), where the Exeter Canal empties into the river.

> **Exeter Canal** This was the first lock canal in the country, originally built in the 16th century and extended to link Exeter with Topsham. In 1675 the canal was further extended and improved, and converted into a ship canal, the oldest in Britain.

At a public footpath sign turn left Ⓐ down to cross a footbridge over a channel. Climb a stile and then continue diagonally right across a low-lying meadow.

On the far side climb two stiles and the intervening footbridge. Follow the path to the left and after crossing a footbridge, the path bends right to continue by a railway embankment on the left. Go through a series of kissing-gates to reach a tarmac track and turn right along it to reach a lane Ⓑ.

Turn right and walk along the lane as far as a right-hand bend and at a public footpath sign keep ahead to cross two footbridges. Continue across meadows, over a succession of footbridges crossing channels, eventually going through a kissing-gate and heading up to the canal towpath **C**. Ahead across the river is historic Topsham, Exeter's port in Roman times. Turn right along the towpath (keeping an eye out for cyclists) and continue to The Turf **A**. The Turf Lock was built in 1827. From here retrace your steps to the start. ●

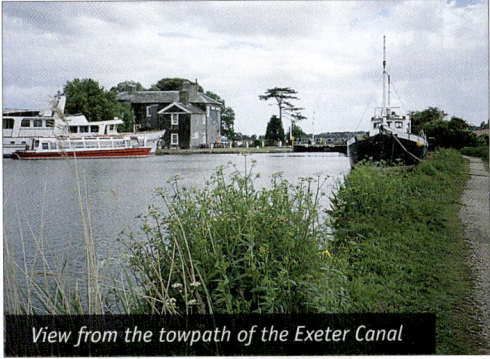
View from the towpath of the Exeter Canal

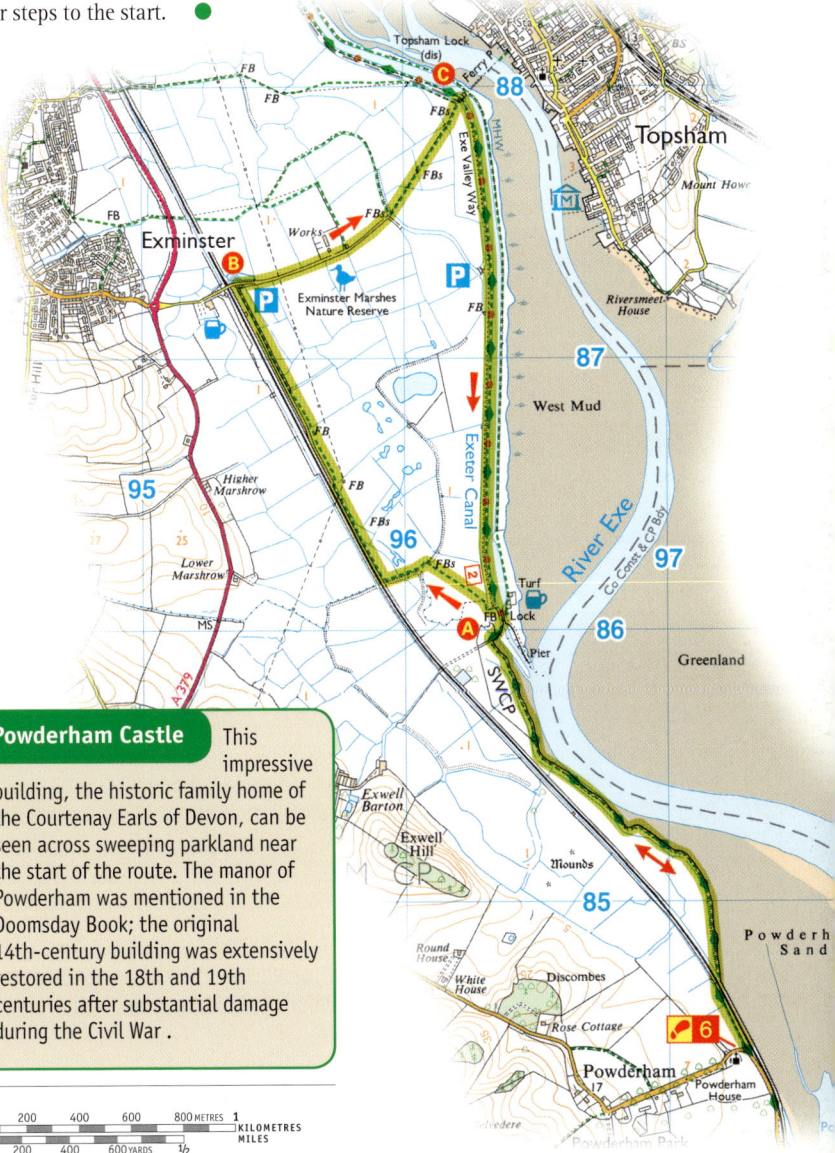

SCALE 1:27777 or about 2½ INCHES to 1 MILE 3.6CM to 1KM

Powderham Castle

This impressive building, the historic family home of the Courtenay Earls of Devon, can be seen across sweeping parkland near the start of the route. The manor of Powderham was mentioned in the Doomsday Book; the original 14th-century building was extensively restored in the 18th and 19th centuries after substantial damage during the Civil War .

walk 7

Start
Noss Mayo

Distance
4½ miles (7.2km)

Height gain
460 feet (140m)

Approximate time
2½ hours

Route terrain
Easy tracks and level Coast Path; steady ascent from start to Ⓐ

Parking
Car park (free) at Noss Mayo 4 miles (6.4km) south-west of Yealmpton

Dog friendly
On lead in farmland

OS maps
Landranger 201 (Plymouth & Launceston) and 202 (Torbay & South Dartmoor), Explorer OL20 (South Devon)

GPS waypoints

SX 547 474
Ⓐ SX 541 466
Ⓑ SX 538 464
Ⓒ SX 547 475

The Yealm Estuary

A great advantage of this walk is that the only real climbing, a steady ¾ mile ascent, comes right at the beginning to reach the coast at The Warren. The rest of the route follows part of Revelstoke Drive, a flat and well-surfaced 9-mile track laid out in the 19th century by Lord Revelstoke, a local landowner. The track follows an outstandingly attractive stretch of the coast before bearing right to continue along the beautiful, wooded shores of the Yealm estuary. On this final part of the walk there are superb views across the water to the houses of Newton Ferrers massed on the opposite shore.

Noss Mayo Noss Mayo, situated on the south side of Newton Creek, an arm of the Yealm estuary, is the twin village of Newton Ferrers on the north side. Both are extremely attractive and photogenic.

Start by turning left out of the car park, at a public footpath sign to 'The Warren', along an uphill lane. The lane continues as a rough track, ascending steadily all the while, and after ¾ mile it reaches a lane. Turn left and take the first turning on the right Ⓐ to pass through The Warren National Trust car park.

At the far end pass through a gate and bear right along a hedge-lined track towards the sea. Climb a stone stile and follow the track to the right and you will shortly pick up the Coast Path Ⓑ. Now comes a delightful stretch of coastal walking along the well-constructed Revelstoke Drive, passing through several gates. The views ahead are most impressive

The Yealm estuary

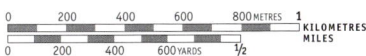
Looking along the coast from Revelstoke Drive

looking towards the estuary of the River Yealm and beyond to Plymouth Sound. The track curves right to keep above the Yealm and later continues through attractive woodland fringing the estuary. On this section there are some gates and stiles, and at intervals gaps in the trees reveal fine views over the water.

Continue along a tarmac drive by the estuary and later beside Newton Creek into Noss Mayo. On the opposite side of the creek, the houses of Newton Ferrers, topped by the church tower, make a very attractive scene. Follow the lane to the right, passing in front of cottages. Continue uphill, passing the waterside **Ship Inn**, and at a junction turn right **C** along a lane with a 'No Through Road' sign to return to the start. ●

SCALE 1:25000 or 2½ INCHES to 1 MILE *4CM to 1KM*

Start

Tipton St John

Distance

5 miles (7.9km)

Height gain

490 feet (150m)

Approximate time

2½ hours

Route terrain

Undulating hedged tracks (some muddy after wet weather), heathland, quiet lanes

P Parking

Tipton St John Playing Fields car park (contributions box), 4¼ miles (6.8km) north-west of Sidmouth

Dog friendly

On lead in lanes and under control in nature reserve

OS maps

Landranger 192 (Exeter & Sidmouth), Explorer 115 (Exmouth & Sidmouth)

GPS waypoints

SY 090 917
Ⓐ SY 085 915
Ⓑ SY 066 915
Ⓒ SY 067 926
Ⓓ SY 087 926
Ⓔ SY 087 921

Venn Ottery Common

From the banks of the River Otter the route climbs steadily and easily, along quiet lanes and enclosed tracks, on to Venn Ottery Common (RSPB reserve). From this elevated expanse of heather and gorse there are tremendous panoramic views over the Otter valley. After descending from the common you continue along more lanes and tracks and there is a short stretch of pleasant riverside walking before returning to the start. This is an undulating walk with no steep or strenuous climbs.

Turn right out of the car park at the bottom end of Tipton St John and cross the bridge over the River Otter. At a T-junction in front of Tipton church, turn left, in the Venn Ottery and Newton Poppleford direction, along a lane which heads uphill and then curves right. Where the lane bends sharply left, keep ahead Ⓐ along a tarmac track with an 'Unsuitable for Motors' road sign. After the tarmac track ends, continue along an enclosed track, between hedgebanks, which gradually ascends and then descends to a lane. Keep ahead, steadily uphill, along the lane and just before the top of the hill, turn right Ⓑ, at a public footpath sign, through a gate into Venn Ottery Common Nature Reserve. Follow the path across the open, heather- and gorse-covered common. As you proceed the views are magnificent, especially to the right over the Otter valley.

Pass a solitary footpath post; descend to a fork where you take the left-hand path which continues more steeply downhill towards woodland. On entering the trees keep ahead to cross a sleeper bridge. Continue to a footbridge over a stream. Cross this and head uphill along a sunken, enclosed path overhung by trees. Turn left on meeting a tarmac drive and take the first turning on the right to follow a hedge-lined track to a road.

Cross over the road, take the lane ahead, signposted 'Broad Oak and West Hill', and at a crossroads turn right Ⓒ, in the Metcombe and Tipton St John direction, heading downhill. Where the lane bends sharply right, keep ahead, at a public footpath sign 'Unmetalled Road'. Where the tarmac track ends, by a thatched cottage, continue along a hedge-lined track. Follow this attractive, undulating track for 1 mile – there are fine views over the valley ahead – eventually descending quite

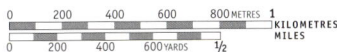

A quiet track below Venn Ottery Common

steeply, passing a track (right) and continuing downhill to reach a road. Turn right and, at a public footpath sign, turn left **D** along a tarmac track which later continues as a rough, hedge-lined track. Follow the track through a gate and then another onto a disused railway line. Contine ahead across a field to the banks of the River Otter.

Turn right alongside the river (Tipton Mill opposite), and follow it as it curves right towards a disused railway bridge. Go under it and continue by the river-bank to a gate. Go through, bear right to cross a footbridge over a stream and continue along a broad, grassy, partially tree-lined track. Go through two gates on to a road **E**, turn left and by the church follow the road to the left to return to the start.

SCALE 1:27777 or about 2¼ INCHES to 1 MILE 3.6CM to 1KM

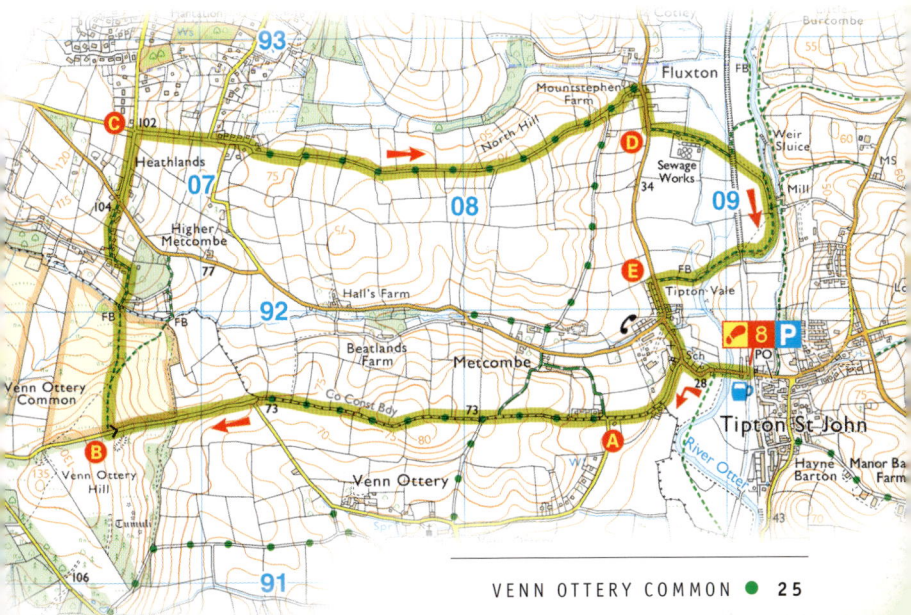

walk 9

Start

Little Dartmouth

Distance

3¾ miles (5.9km)

Height gain

720 feet (220m)

Approximate time

2½ hours

Route terrain

Fields and undulating
Coast Path

P Parking

National Trust car park
at Little Dartmouth,
2½ miles (4km) south
of Dartmouth off
B3205

Dog friendly

On lead in farmland;
stretches of unfenced
cliff

OS maps

Landranger 202
(Torbay & South
Dartmoor), Explorer
OL20 (South Devon)

GPS waypoints

🖊 SX 874 491
Ⓐ SX 876 486
Ⓑ SX 884 500
Ⓒ SX 886 502

Dart Estuary and Dartmouth Castle

Although only a short walk, this is quite an energetic one with plenty of ascents and descents as you follow a rugged stretch of coast around Compass Cove and Blackstone Point, to continue through woodland above the Dart estuary to Dartmouth Castle. Both on the first part of the walk and on the return inland leg, there are superb views along the coast and across the estuary to the castle at Kingswear.

⚠ Sections of this walk are quite exposed with sheer drops from the cliff, so care should be taken.

🖊 Facing the sea, walk to the right-hand corner of the car park where you go through a kissing-gate to the right of an information board. Take the path ahead along the right edge of fields, by a hedge, go through a gate and descend gently to a kissing-gate. Go through and turn left Ⓐ to follow the Coast Path to Dartmouth Castle.

This is a highly attractive walk and easy to follow as you keep along the winding, up-and-down path, looking out for the regular acorn symbols and passing through several gates. The views are superb as the path proceeds around Warren Point and Combe Point, to Compass Cove. Soon after a right curve at Compass Cove, the path turns right downhill towards the sea, later bearing right at the bottom to a stile. Climb it, turn left and descend steps to a rocky cove. Cross a footbridge over a small inlet and the path bends left around Blackstone Point to continue by the Dart estuary, with striking views of Kingswear

Dartmouth Castle

Castle on the opposite shore. It later climbs through woodland.

Go through a gate and continue through the beautiful sloping woodland, eventually heading up to a T-junction **B** by a fingerpost in front of a house, Compass Cottage. Turn right, in the Dartmouth direction, along a tarmac track and at a waymarked post a few yards ahead, bear right and head downhill along a path through trees. Look out for another waymarked post which directs you to turn sharp right and follow a zigzag path down a flight of steps. Later the route continues up steps to eventually emerge onto a lane by a parking area. Turn right and descend more steps to Dartmouth Castle and **tearoom C**, about 1 mile south of the town centre.

From the castle, retrace your route up steps (on the Coast Path) to the lane, turn left and continue up a tarmac track to the fingerpost at Compass Cottage **B**, briefly rejoining the outward route here. Keep ahead, following the signs 'Bridleway, Little Dartmouth'. Continue uphill, along a track which runs through woodland. Go through a gate, continue along the track and where it ends go through a kissing-gate, at a National Trust 'Little Dartmouth' sign. Walk along a path, by a hedge on the right-hand side, which curves left up to a gate, go through and continue along an enclosed track, passing through the farmyard of Little Dartmouth, to return to the start.

Dartmouth Castle

Like its counterpart at Kingswear, it was built in the late 15th century to guard the entrance to Dartmouth harbour and is the earliest artillery fort in the country. As an additional defence, a chain could be hung across the estuary between the two castles. Within the precincts is the mainly 17th-century church of St Petrox, whose tower dominates most views.

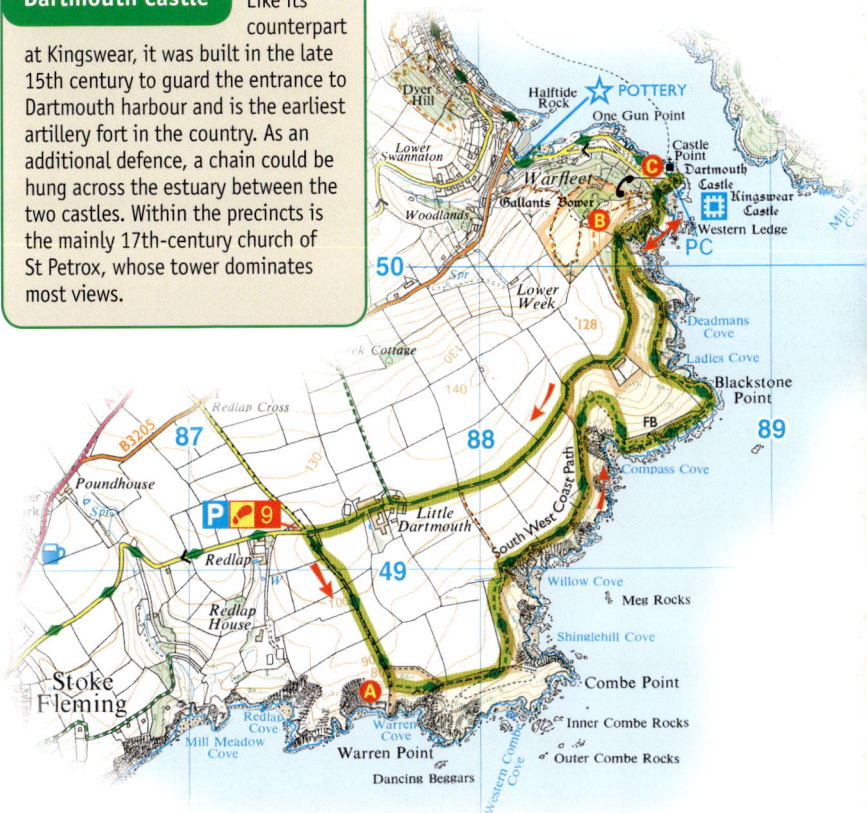

SCALE 1:25000 or 2½ INCHES to 1 MILE 4CM to 1KM

Broadhembury

Start

Broadhembury

Distance

4½ miles (7.2km)

Height gain

590 feet (180m)

Approximate time

2½ hours

Route terrain

Field and woodland paths; steady climb from start to **Ⓐ**

P Parking

In the village square at Broadhembury (free), 5¼ miles (8.4km) north-west of Honiton

Dog friendly

On lead in farmland

OS maps

Landranger 192 (Exeter & Sidmouth), Explorer 115 (Exmouth & Sidmouth)

GPS waypoints

⬙ ST 101 047
Ⓐ ST 117 053
Ⓑ ST 115 066
Ⓒ ST 102 063
Ⓓ ST 100 051

Starting in one of the prettiest villages in East Devon, the route heads uphill along a lane on to a steep, wooded ridge and follows this ridge as it curves left around the head of a combe. On this part of the walk there are outstanding views over a rolling and well-wooded landscape. The descent, along enclosed tracks and field paths, across fields and through woodland, provides some fine views of Broadhembury village and church. Parts of the walk are likely to be muddy after wet weather.

Broadhembury Thatched and colour-washed cottages (many dating from the 17th century) with colourful gardens, an old inn on the village square, a sparkling stream and a medieval church, all combine to make Broadhembury an exceptionally attractive and unspoilt village. The mainly 14th and 15th-century church is distinguished by its tall west tower, a landmark from several points on the walk.

⬙ Start in the square and turn up the lane which passes to the left of the war memorial. Keep along this lane for 1¼ miles, following signs to Dunkerswell and Sheldon, heading uphill. After several steep bends the road continues to climb through woodland and, where it eventually bends right, turn left **Ⓐ**, at a public bridleway sign, to go on to a path.

The path, which is lined with bluebells in spring, keeps along the right inside edge of sloping conifer woodland. Go through two gates. After the second one, keep ahead to join a track and bear left along it to go through a metal gate. Continue across a sloping field, then bear left to join and follow a wire fence and a line of trees on the left to a metal gate. Go through the gate, continue along an enclosed, hedge and tree-lined path, and, on emerging from the trees, superb views open up to the left over rolling, wooded country.

After going through the next gate, in a line of beech trees, turn right along a fence-lined track and go through another gate onto a lane. Turn left and, after about 200 yds, turn left again **Ⓑ** along the tree-lined, tarmac drive of the Devon and Somerset Gliding Club. Soon after emerging from the trees, go through a gate beside a cattle-grid and follow the drive to the left. Pass some of the club's hangars and turn right to continue along the left edge of the airfield. Later the tarmac drive

Main street, Broadhembury

becomes a rough track that runs parallel to a wire fence bordering woodland on the left. Keep ahead to eventually reach a bridle-path junction; turn left here **C**, just before a big stand of gorse, to pass through a metal gate. Follow a path downhill through woodland, soon passing through an old iron gate. Broadhembury church can be seen through gaps in the trees.

Continue along a sunken track and, after a few yards, turn left over a stile, bear slightly right and head across a field to climb a stile into more woodland. After going through a small copse, climb another stile, continue gently downhill along the left edge of a field and turn left over a stile in the bottom corner.

Walk along an enclosed path, climb a stile and continue along what is now a wider enclosed track to climb another stile. Keep ahead downhill across the field to another stile. Climb it, keep along the right edge of the next field, by a wire fence and hedge on the right, and where the fence and hedge bend right, keep ahead across the field and climb a stile onto a lane. Turn right **D** and follow the lane back to Broadhembury. The lane bears right beside the little River Tale; turn left over a bridge to return to the start and **The Drewe Arms**. ●

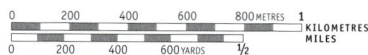

SCALE 1:25000 or 2½ INCHES to 1 MILE 4CM to 1KM

0	200	400	600	800 METRES	1
					KILOMETRES
					MILES
0	200	400	600 YARDS		½

Overlooking Brixham Harbour

Slightly harder walks of 3 – 3½ hours

Loddiswell and the Avon Valley Woods

Start
Loddiswell

Distance
5¼ miles (8.3km)

Height gain
425 feet (130m)

Approximate time
3 hours

Route terrain
Fields, riverside tracks and paths, some muddy and uneven; many high stiles; steady climb to finish

P Parking
Car park in Loddiswell (free), 3½ miles (5.6km) north of Kingsbridge

Dog friendly
On lead in farmland and Avon Woods

OS maps
Landranger 202 (Torbay & South Devon), Explorer OL20 (South Devon)

GPS waypoints
SX 720 485
Ⓐ SX 719 483
Ⓑ SX 714 472
Ⓒ SX 717 470
Ⓓ SX 719 478
Ⓔ SX 731 483
Ⓕ SX 731 495

From Loddiswell the route descends across fields into the Avon valley and continues through it, keeping close to the river. The undoubted highlight of the walk is a delightful ramble through the Avon Valley Woodlands that clothe the steep-sided, eastern slopes of the valley, one of the largest areas of woodland in the South Hams. After doubling back to continue through more beautiful woodland on the west bank of the Avon, a steady climb leads back to the start.

Loddiswell Loddiswell is a hilltop village situated high above the western side of the Avon valley. Close to the village centre is the attractive, mainly 14th- to 15th-century church.

The walk starts in the village centre. With your back to the **Loddiswell Inn** take the main road ahead through the village. Keep ahead where the road bends left and on the next left bend, by the school, turn right Ⓐ along Towns Lane. The lane leads gently uphill and where it bends right, keep ahead over a stile, at a public footpath sign.

Walk along the left edge of a field, cross a stile and continue along the left edge of the next. Cross another stile. Ahead are attractive views over the gently rolling landscape of the Avon valley. After the third stile head downhill across the middle of a field, cross a waymarked stile by a gate, and continue down along the right edge of a field. Look out for a waymark that directs you over a stile by a gate on the right. Bear left down the next field, keeping to the right of ponds in the middle, to reach a stone stile. Climb it and turn left on to a sunken, enclosed track – likely to be muddy – to a lane to the right of Hatch Bridge Ⓑ.

Turn left to cross the bridge over the River Avon. Continue along the tree-lined lane and at a public footpath sign just before the second turning on the right, turn left Ⓒ over a stile. Keep ahead across a field, bear left to cross a footbridge over a stream and continue across the field to join and keep beside the riverbank. Climb a stile, immediately cross a ditch and continue beside the Avon to New Bridge where you turn right up steps to a road. Cross over, turn left down the steps opposite and continue by the river. Climb a stile in a field corner to reach a lane by Newmill Bridge **D**.

Do not cross the bridge; keep ahead along the lane. Turn left at the sign for **Avon Mill Garden Centre & Café**, then right over a stile before the bridge on a footpath that follows the river again. Rejoin the lane via a stile. Pass under a disused railway bridge after which the lane bears to the left, and, soon after it bears right, keep ahead over a stile **E** just to the right of the former Loddiswell station. The station was on a branch line that ran from South Brent on the edge of Dartmoor to Kingsbridge before its closure in 1963. Take the path ahead and soon after it enters woodland you reach a stile on the left.

At this point you have a choice of routes. Either keep ahead along the undulating path and, by a waymarked post where you see an old railway bridge over to the left, turn left to join a track and turn right over that bridge. Alternatively turn left over the stile and turn right

along the disused railway track – this is a permissive route – keeping parallel to the river to reach the bridge. Either way it is a delightful walk through the Avon Valley Woodlands, owned and managed by the Woodland Trust for public enjoyment and recreation.

After crossing the bridge immediately turn left **F** down steps. After a few yards reach a footpath junction; take the left fork to follow a well-waymarked path back along the other bank of the Avon, climbing a number of stiles. The

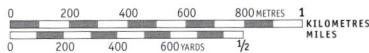

SCALE 1:25000 or 2½ INCHES to 1 MILE 4CM to 1KM

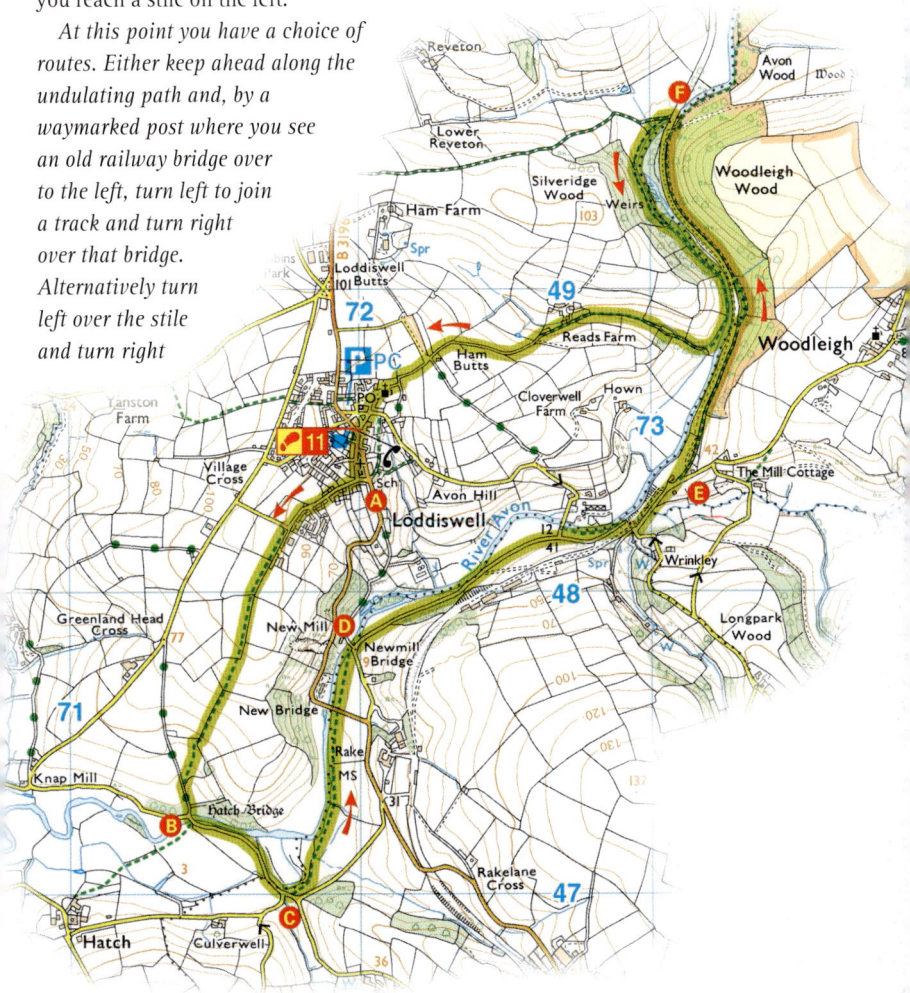

route proceeds through more beautiful woodland, with one intervening meadow, crosses several footbridges over side streams and keeps close to the river which flows through what is virtually a thickly wooded gorge.

Eventually the path emerges from the woods to continue across a meadow to a public footpath sign at the far end. Turn right along a path which runs beside a stream on the left, turn left over a footbridge and then turn right to continue along a sunken, enclosed path, now with the stream on the right. Keep ahead, eventually crossing a stile, and continue gently uphill before going through a metal gate on to a tarmac track. Keep ahead along the steadily ascending lane into Loddiswell, passing to the right of the church. Bear left between cottages, then right on the lane to regain the start. ●

The River Avon near Loddiswell

Ashburton and Whiddon Scrubbs

After an initial walk across fields by the little River Ashburn, the route climbs steadily through the delightful woodland of Whiddon Scrubbs to Owlacombe Cross. The descent, via a lane and farm tracks, leads back to the edge of Ashburton for the grand finale, the high-level Terrace Walk from which there are splendid views over the southern fringes of Dartmoor.

Start
Ashburton Town Hall

Distance
5½ miles (8.8km)

Height gain
655 feet (200m)

Approximate time
3 hours

Route terrain
Woodland paths, fields, rural lanes; steady ascent from **C**

Parking
Ashburton
(pay & display)

Dog friendly
On lead in farmland and at Lower Whiddon

OS maps
Landrangers 202 (Torbay & South Devon) and 191 (Okehampton & North Dartmoor), Explorer OL28 (Dartmoor)

GPS waypoints
- SX 755 699
- **A** SX 754 702
- **B** SX 758 709
- **C** SX 753 719
- **D** SX 764 726
- **E** SX 771 719
- **F** SX 765 709
- **G** SX 760 705

Ashburton Ashburton is an attractive and unspoilt little town with many old gabled and slate-fronted buildings. In the Middle Ages it was one of the four stannary towns (from the Latin *stannum* meaning tin), an administrative centre for the flourishing tin-mining industry on Dartmoor at the time. In addition it was an important cloth making town. Its medieval prosperity is reflected in buildings such as the handsome 15th-century church with its imposing tower, and the restored St Lawrence's Chapel which in the past has served as a chantry chapel, school and courtroom. Despite its modest size, Ashburton is the largest town within the National Park and makes a good base from which to explore southern Dartmoor.

The walk starts from the Town Hall in the centre of Ashburton. With the Town Hall on your left walk up North Street. After just under ¼ mile – opposite Crockaton Cottages – look for a public footpath sign to 'Terrace Walk' **A**, turn right up steps and go through an iron kissing-gate at another public footpath sign. Continue, in the Cuddyford Cross direction, along the bottom edge of a sloping field, eventually parallel to the little River Ashburn on the left, to a stone stile. Climb it and continue by the tree-lined river. At the end of the field bear away from the river to climb another stone stile and descend steps to a lane **B**.

Cross over, climb steps opposite at a public footpath sign, go through an iron kissing-gate and bear left along the left edge of a field, by a hedge on the left. Climb a stile, continue along an enclosed, hedge-lined path, climb another stile and cross a stream. The path continues along the bottom inside edge of sloping woodland to a fingerpost. Climb a stile by a gate and keep ahead on an attractive stretch of the walk as you bear left

South Devons on Terrace Walk

along the bottom edge of Whiddon Scrubbs beside the River Ashburn. Go through a metal kissing-gate, keep ahead and just before reaching a footbridge over the river and lane beyond, turn right, at a public footpath sign to Owlacombe, on to an uphill track **C**.

Initially the track continues through woodland; later it becomes enclosed between hedges and heads steadily uphill to farm buildings. At a T-junction by the farm, turn right on to a tarmac drive which curves left and heads up to emerge on to a lane **D** just south of Owlacombe Cross. Turn right, and at a

fork continue steeply downhill along the left-hand lane. Soon after a high wall (right) turn right **E** at a public footpath sign along the tarmac, hedge-lined track to Waye House. In front of the large house turn left, in the direction of Waye Farm. Head downhill and at a fork just before the farm take the left-hand track, and continue steadily downhill.

From now on the noise of traffic on the busy A38 can be heard. The track flattens out by a quarry on the left. Keep ahead and where the track ends in front of a large house bear left as signed to pass through a kissing-gate. Follow the fenced path to pass in front of the house, then by a school car park (right), and eventually through a kissing-gate. Descend some steps and turn right to reach a lane **F**. Turn right and after a few yards take the first turning on the right (Place Lane), running past South Dartmoor Community College. Follow the lane around left and right bends to reach a crossroads and then turn left to go through a suburban housing area on the edge of Ashburton.

Where a footpath crosses over the road (just before a sign 'Higher Roborough' on the left), turn right **G** along a narrow path, with a wall

right, which continues up between hedgebanks to an iron kissing-gate. Go through and on along the Terrace Walk, a flat, grassy path that follows the contours of the side of the hill giving fine views over the southern edge of Dartmoor and providing a superb end to the walk. Rejoin the outward route by an iron kissing-gate. From here retrace your steps to the start. ●

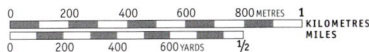

SCALE 1:25 000 or 2½ INCHES to 1 MILE 4CM to 1KM

Start

Trenchford Reservoir

Distance

5¾ miles (9.1km)

Height gain

460 feet (140m)

Approximate time

3 hours

Route terrain

Quiet rural lanes,
fields, woodland paths

P Parking

Trenchford Reservoir
picnic site at Bullaton
Cross, 3 miles (4.8km)
north of Bovey Tracey

Dog friendly

On lead in farmland
and in Clampitt
Plantation (chickens)

OS maps

Landranger 191
(Okehampton & North
Dartmoor), Explorer
110 (Torquay &
Dawlish)

GPS waypoints

SX 804 823
Ⓐ SX 813 826
Ⓑ SX 824 839
Ⓒ SX 819 847
Ⓓ SX 811 843
Ⓔ SX 807 838
Ⓕ SX 803 834

Three Reservoirs Walk

The three adjacent reservoirs of Trenchford, Tottiford and Kennick lie in secluded, rolling and well-wooded country on the eastern fringes of Dartmoor. They were constructed between 1860 and 1907 to serve the rapidly growing resorts of Torbay. This easy-paced walk links them via quiet lanes (the banks carpeted with wildflowers), fields and woodland tracks, passing stands of beech and conifer, with fine views across the water.

From the car park pass a sign for 'Picnic Area/Walks' down steps. Pass picnic tables and then a small granite building marking the intake from Fernworthy Reservoir on the High Moor. Turn left on the lane to cross the dam. Where it bends left between Trenchford and Tottiford reservoirs, bear right along a tarmac track to a T-junction. Turn left Ⓐ along a quiet lane, with lovely views right, for ¾ mile, heading gently uphill to another junction. Turn right (Christow). Ignore a left turn to Bridford; continue, bearing left along the next narrow lane reached.

At a public footpath sign turn left Ⓑ over a stile and bear left across rough pasture, heading gently downhill to a fingerpost at the field edge. Turn right along the left edge of the field. Keep the wire fence on the left and follow the path, which

Kennick Reservoir

SCALE 1:25000 or 2½ INCHES to 1 MILE 4CM to 1KM

0	200	400	600	800 METRES	1
					KILOMETRES
					MILES

0	200	400	600 YARDS	½

head across the field and go through another metal gate on to a lane **C**. Turn left and, at a meeting of lanes, keep straight ahead, by a 'No Through Road' symbol, along an enclosed, tarmac track, heading uphill. This track becomes rougher, and continues through conifer plantations. Eventually keep ahead downhill, in the Kennick direction, along an attractive, tree-lined track to a T-junction where a plaque marks the Clampitt Quakers Burial Ground (1674–1740). At the time, an age of religious intolerance, the Quakers had to hold their meetings in secluded places like this to avoid persecution.

Turn left **D** along a track, at the next T-junction follow the track to the right and, at a fingerpost a few yards on keep ahead, signed Kennick Reservoir, descending gently through conifers. Keep ahead at a fingerpost eventually to pass through a kissing-gate on to a lane. Turn right to Kennick Reservoir. The view across the water to the right is particularly attractive. On reaching the corner of the reservoir turn left **E**

eventually leads into trees, following yellow arrows. On reaching the end of the wood follow the fence right, and a few yards ahead turn left through a metal gate. Head round the right edge of a field, passing through a kissing-gate on the far side. Continue along the right edge of the next field, following the fence round to the right to go through a metal gate by farm buildings. Turn left along a track, turn left again through the first metal gate and walk slightly uphill along the left edge of a field. By a metal gate and public footpath sign on the left, turn right to

Bluebell bank, Tottiford

through a gate, at a 'Tottiford Walk' sign, and continue along a path which descends through trees to reach the north end of Tottiford Reservoir, at which point another attractive scene unfolds.

Turn right at a small footpath post to cross the end of the reservoir on a small bridge, and follow the path to the left alongside it. Look out for an uphill path leading right, signed to Trenchford; climb through woodland to pass through a kissing-gate on to a lane. Turn left and almost immediately right, through a gate **F**, at a sign to Trenchford Reservoir, along a path

under conifers. Follow the direction of a waymarked post to the left and look out for the next post which directs you to bear right. Continue gently downhill, cross a footbridge over a stream and the path now bends left to reach the side of a footbridge at the end of Trenchford Reservoir.

At a fingerpost keep ahead, in the 'Trenchford Walk, to Car Park' direction, along a path which bends to the left across a boardwalk and continues along the right edge of the reservoir. Later the path bears right and heads gently uphill through woodland to return to the start. ●

Brixham and Churston Point

From Brixham Harbour the route follows an attractive and well-wooded stretch of coast, via Churston Cove and Elberry Cove, rounding Churston Point to reach the sandy bay of Broadsands. The return leg takes a pleasant inland route, passing Churston Court and church, and regains the Coast Path at Churston Cove for the final ¾ mile back to Brixham. The shorter version returns from Elberry Cove.

Start
Brixham Harbour

Distance
6 miles (9.5km), shorter version 5½ miles(8.5km)

Height gain
525 feet (160m), shorter version 475 feet (145m)

Approximate time
3 hours, shorter version 2½ hours

Route terrain
Tarmac paths, well-used Coast Path, woodland tracks

P **Parking**
Brixham (pay & display)

Dog friendly
Under control in Brixham and on golf course

OS maps
Landranger 202 (Torbay & South Dartmoor), Explorer OL20 (South Devon)

GPS waypoints
  SX 925 562
Ⓐ SX 918 568
Ⓑ SX 901 570
Ⓒ SX 898 572
Ⓓ SX 900 567
Ⓔ SX 905 562

Brixham For generations of holidaymakers at the nearby resorts of Torbay, a boat trip across the bay to Brixham has always been an essential and highly enjoyable part of the holiday. Despite more recent development as a busy resort, Brixham is still a working port and retains the atmosphere of a traditional fishing village, with narrow streets and rows of colourful houses and cottages rising steeply from the harbour. In 1688 Brixham played a major role in the development of British history when William of Orange landed here to begin his successful campaign to win the throne from his father-in-law, James II. His statue by the harbour is the starting point for the walk.

Face the sea and walk along the left side of the harbour. Where the road bends left uphill, bear right and then left, at a Coast Path sign, and take the winding path at first beside the the Fish Market then Outer Harbour and later along the right edge of a large car park. At the far end continue along a tarmac path to a Coast Path sign, climb some steps and at a fork take the left-hand path that ascends into woodland, eventually reaching a road.

Brixham

Turn right; pass a sign to Fishcombe Cove (right) and keep ahead along an enclosed path. The path turns left through a metal kissing-gate to a fingerpost and junction of paths **Ⓐ**. Bear right, in the Churston Cove direction, between trees and follow Coast Path signs left and then right, then down steep steps and along the edge of Churston Cove. Cross the stony beach. On the other side climb some steps to continue through delightful woodland by Fishcombe Point. Later the path bends right, curves downhill and descends more steps to reach Elberry Cove. Walk across the beach and ascend the steps on the far side to reach a path junction **Ⓑ**.

At this point the shorter version takes the sharp turning on the left along a path which curves right, continues between hedges and bears left to meet a

Brixham's Outer Harbour from Churston Cove

track coming in from the right. Keep ahead here to rejoin the full walk.

For the full walk keep ahead, pass through a metal kissing-gate and continue along the right edge of an open grassy area around Churston Point. After passing through another metal kissing-gate, a tarmac path curves left alongside the wide, sandy expanses of Broadsands. Keep ahead along the left edge of a car park, bearing left to a footpath signpost, and turn left **C** along a tarmac track. After passing to the left of Elberry Farm, this becomes a rough track which continues to a T-junction, here rejoining the shorter version.

Turn right along a track, climb a metal stile/kissing-gate and continue along a hedge-lined path which heads gently uphill into trees. Take the first turning on the left **D**, go through a wall gap and continue through trees and later bracken. Follow the path across a golf course, keeping between the lines of yellow posts, and on the far side go through a metal kissing-gate. Keep along an enclosed, tree-lined

path, turn right at a T-junction and after a few yards turn left along a lane to emerge on to another. Continue along the lane which bends right beside the Church of St Mary the Virgin. The medieval church and 17th-century **Churston Court** standing side by side make an attractive and traditional composition. The church was originally the private chapel of the house which is now an inn.

Follow the lane to the left; at a junction bear slightly left and after a few yards turn left over a stone stile beside a metal gate **E**. Continue along a hedge-lined track. After skirting woodland on the left the track bears right over a stone stile by a metal gate. Walk across a field and on the far side follow the path through woodland and occasional grassy glades. Keep on the main path all the time, eventually descending to a junction of paths by a fingerpost **A**. Turn right through a metal kissing-gate to pick up the outward route and then retrace your steps to the start.

SCALE 1:27777 or about 2¼ INCHES to 1 MILE 3.6CM to 1KM

0	200	400	600	800 METRES	1
					KILOMETRES
					MILES
0	200	400	600 YARDS	½	

walk 15

Start
Prawle Point

Distance
5¾ miles (9.1km)

Height gain
690 feet (210m)

Approximate time
3 hours

Route terrain
Field paths, rocky and undulating Coast Path

Parking
National Trust car park (honesty box) at Prawle Point, just over 1 mile (1.6km) south-west of East Prawle

Dog friendly
On lead in coastal fields (livestock)

OS maps
Landranger 202 (Torbay & South Dartmoor), Explorer OL20 (South Devon)

GPS waypoints
- SX 774 354
- Ⓐ SX 766 358
- Ⓑ SX 767 361
- Ⓒ SX 780 363
- Ⓓ SX 786 371
- Ⓔ SX 794 369

Prawle Point and Woodcombe Point

Prawle Point is the southernmost tip of Devon and is situated amid some of the most dramatic coastal scenery in southern England. The walk starts by passing the Point and continuing along the coastline almost to Gammon Head. Then follows an inland section, mainly along enclosed paths and tracks, passing through the village of East Prawle and rejoining the coast at Woodcombe Sand. The final part of the route from Woodcombe Point to Prawle Point provides coastal walking at its finest.

Gammon Head from Prawle Point

Climb a stile by the car park entrance, walk downhill along the right-hand edge of a field to a fingerpost and turn right through a gate to join the Coast Path. Now comes a spectacular stretch of coastal walking: the path winds around this wild and rugged coastline, passing Prawle Point (call into the National Coastguard Watch visitor centre) and continuing around Elender Cove, with the jagged profile of Gammon Head visible ahead. There are several gates and stiles,

but follow the yellow waymarks and acorn symbols all the time.

At a waymarked post above Maceley Cove turn right **A**. Head up to the next waymarked post and turn left. Continue steadily uphill, go through a gate, and at a junction of paths and tracks turn right along an enclosed track **B**. Keep along this to a lane. Follow the lane as it heads uphill and curves left into East Prawle.

In the village centre turn right **C** in front of the **Pig's Nose Inn** and follow a lane to the left. Take the first turning on the right, continue along a curving lane heading uphill, and just in front of a telephone box turn right along a tarmac track. This later becomes a rough track, enclosed between high hedges, and passes the drive to Maelcombe House. Follow the track down into and out of a wooded area, then along the left edge of a field to a metal gate. Go through and turn right along a tarmac track **D**, at a public bridleway sign to Lannacombe Green and Woodcombe Sand. Follow the track around a left bend and where the tarmac way bends right, keep ahead, at a public footpath/bridleway sign, along a grassy, enclosed track. At a fingerpost turn right, in the direction of

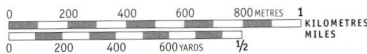

SCALE 1:25000 or 2½ INCHES to 1 MILE 4CM to 1KM

```
0    200   400   600   800 METRES  1
                                    | KILOMETRES
                                    | MILES
0    200   400   600 YARDS    ½
```

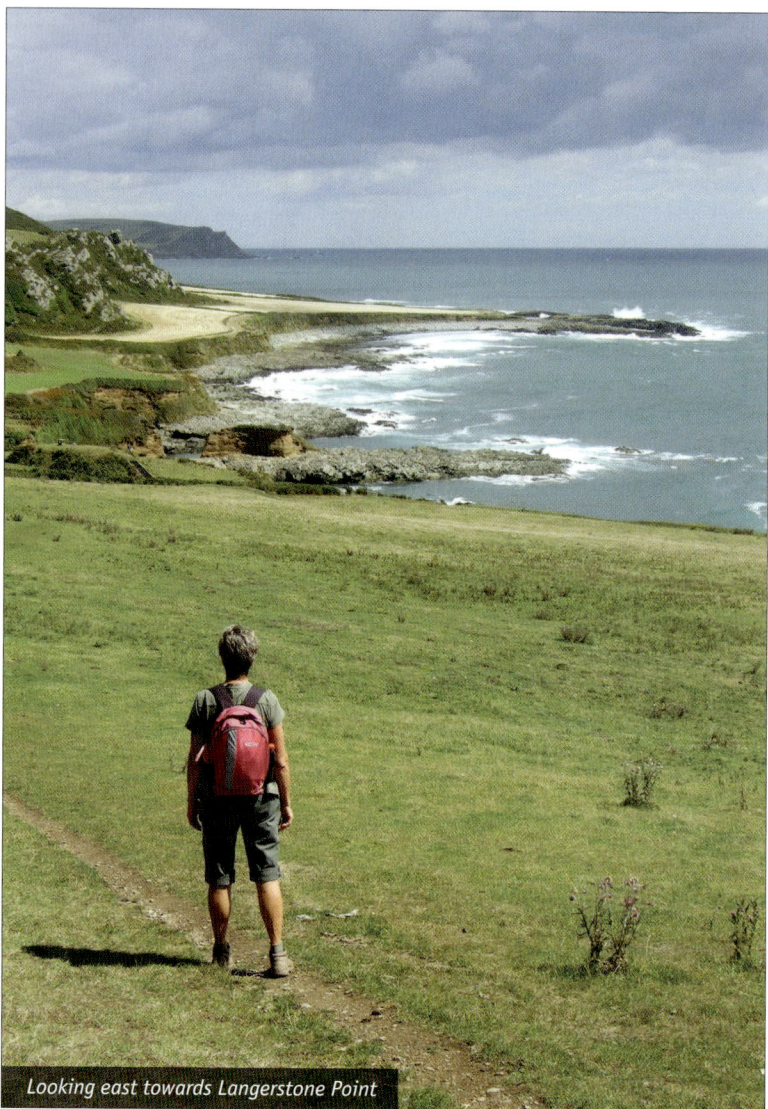

Looking east towards Langerstone Point

Woodcombe Sand, to continue along a most attractive enclosed path. After going through a gate, the path descends quite steeply through trees along the right side of a combe. Follow the path as it bends sharp left and drops to a T-junction of paths above Woodcombe Sand.

Turn right **E** to rejoin the Coast Path, initially between bracken and bushes below Woodcombe Point. Start Point can be seen to the left. Keep along the Coast Path back to the start, negotiating several gates and following the regular acorn symbol waymarks. In particular look out for a sharp left turn, in the Prawle Point direction, and follow the field edge to the right to continue towards Langerstone Point. Pass below it and soon Prawle Point is seen. Keep along the Coast Path as far as a fingerpost in front of a gate, turn right, on a public byway to East Prawle, and retrace your steps to the car park. ●

Otter Estuary, East Budleigh and Otterton

walk 16

Start
Budleigh Salterton

Distance
6¾ miles (10.6km)

Height gain
150 feet (45m)

Approximate time
3 hours

Route terrain
Easy tracks and paths

Parking
Lime Kiln car park (pay & display) at the east end of seafront, Budleigh Salterton

Dog friendly
On lead in farmland

OS maps
Landranger 192 (Exeter & Sidmouth), Explorer 115 (Exmouth & Sidmouth)

GPS waypoints
⬈ SY 072 820
Ⓐ SY 075 839
Ⓑ SY 069 843
Ⓒ SY 067 849
Ⓓ SY 067 854
Ⓔ SY 073 857
Ⓕ SY 078 852

Starting by the Otter estuary, the first part of the route is across riverside meadows. The shorter version returns along the river, but the full walk heads across to the picturesque village of East Budleigh, continues on to Bicton church and rejoins the river at Otterton. The rest of the route is a pleasant and relaxing stroll beside the Otter. This is an easy walk with very little uphill work.

> ### Budleigh Salterton
> The pleasant little resort of Budleigh Salterton, which first developed during the Victorian era, has a fine beach and all the usual seaside amenities.

⬈ From the entrance to the car park turn right, at a Coast Path acorn post, along a path with a stream on the left. By the playground entrance turn left, and after a few yards turn right, at a public footpath sign 'White Bridge', along a path which is initially hedge-lined but later continues below the wooded embankment of a disused railway on the left. This is an attractive part of the walk with fine views across the meadows on the right.

Keep ahead all the while, negotiating several gates and stiles, and crossing a lane. Keep ahead, and the path widens into a track, which eventually bends left. At this point keep ahead, by a waymarked post, over a stile and across grass to another stile. Turn right along a track, which curves right towards the river to meet a footpath post Ⓐ.

For the shorter version turn right here, through a kissing-gate, and follow the riverside path.

The full walk continues by turning left over a stone aqueduct, raised above the low-lying fields to reduce flooding. Immediately over the aqueduct take the left fork, which leads along the top of a raised embankment above the riverside meadows, curving left to a kissing-gate. Climb this, and continue along a narrow, tree-lined path, to join a track. Turn right to reach a lane opposite a large farmhouse. Turn left along the lane to meet a road opposite **The Rolle Arms** Ⓑ. Cross over

The attractive village of East Budleigh

great care – this is a fast road and there is no pavement.

At a public footpath sign opposite Bicton church, bear right **E** along a path, by a wall on the right, that heads down and bears right to continue as a hedge-lined, enclosed path. Cross a farm drive and keep ahead, later turning left and

and keep ahead through East Budleigh. This is a very attractive village with thatched cottages, a stream, and an impressive medieval church that has a pew used by the Raleigh family. Sir Walter Raleigh was born nearby.

The road winds through the village, passing to the right of the church. At the statue of Sir Walter Raleigh turn right in the Newton Poppleford direction. At a public footpath sign **C** turn left up some steps and go through a kissing-gate. Continue along an enclosed path which passes along the left edge of a playing field and curves right to a kissing-gate. Climb this, keep along the right edge of a field, and go through a kissing-gate on to a lane. Turn left and after about 200 yds look out for a waymarked stile on the right **D**. Climb it, walk along the right edge of a field, descending into a dip, and turn right through a gate – there are blue waymarks – to continue along the left edge of a sloping field, by a line of trees on the left. The field edge curves left to meet a track; keep along it, bearing right to a road.

Just before reaching the road turn left down a walled tarmac drive to see Bicton church. Walk back up the walled tarmac drive and turn left to meet the road. *Turn left along the road, taking*

> ### Bicton church
>
> Both the church and the Rolle mausoleum next to it were built in the mid-19th century and there are also the scanty remains of the church's medieval predecessor. Beyond are the gardens of Bicton Park, laid out by the Rolle family. They are open to the public and are well worth a visit. The 18th-century Bicton House is now home to Bicton College.

crossing a footbridge over a stream and then the disused railway line. Continue along the left edge of a field and go through a kissing-gate on to a road. Bear to the left and cross a bridge over a stream. Keep ahead over Otterton Bridge to visit the village of Otterton with its row of thatched cottages, restored **Otterton Mill** (open to the public as a working museum, bakery, craft shop, Devon food shop and restaurant) and 19th-century church.

Return to the bridge, cross over and turn left **F** at a public footpath sign to Budleigh Salterton. Go down some steps and continue along a beautiful riverside path. Go through a kissing-gate by a metal bridge and continue beside the

River Otter, momentarily joining the outward route to cross the stone aqueduct passed earlier **A**. Bear left through a kissing-gate, joining the shorter walk, for another stretch of attractive riverside walking, passing through several more kissing-gates and crossing a lane en route. Eventually the path bears slightly right away from the estuary, rising above the surrounding marshes and creeks, and, after going through the last gate, continues directly back to the car park. ●

Pebble Beds

Budleigh also sits on the 95-mile-long Jurassic Coast World Heritage Site (the first national site to be designated, late 2001). To the west of the seafront are Budleigh's famous Pebble Beds, comprised of water-borne pebbles dating from the Triassic Period, 240 million years ago.

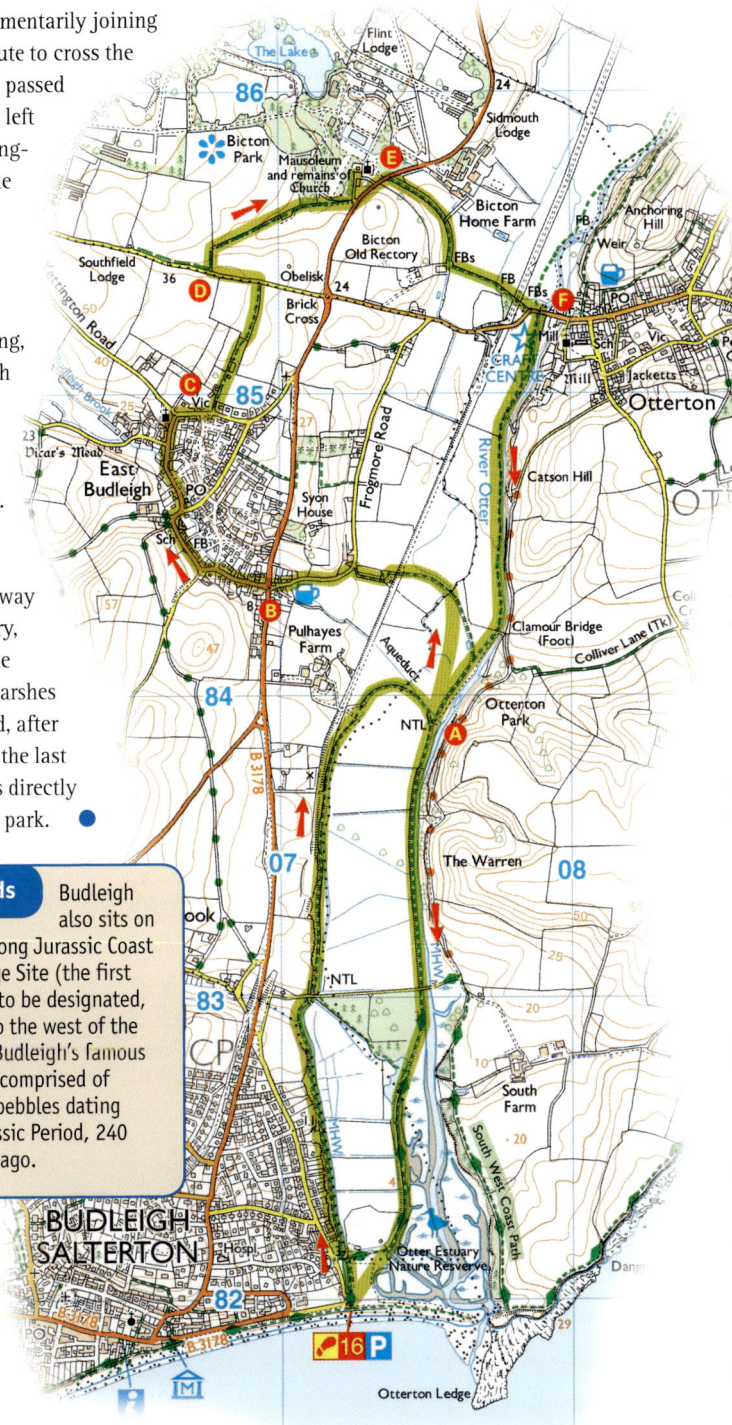

SCALE 1:25000 or 2½ INCHES to 1 MILE 4CM to 1KM

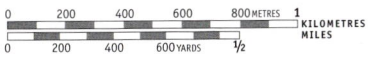

SCALE 1:25000 or 2½ INCHES to 1 MILE 4CM to 1KM

| 0 | 200 | 400 | 600 | 800 METRES | 1 |
KILOMETRES
MILES
| 0 | 200 | 400 | 600 YARDS | ½ |

walk 17

Start
Kingston

Distance
5¾ miles (9.1km)

Height gain
1,035 feet (315m)

Approximate time
3 hours

Route terrain
Field paths, undulating Coast Path; steep and taxing descents to River Erme and Westcombe Beach; track near Okenbury often muddy

Parking
Parking area (free) by St James the Less Church, Kingston, 4½ miles (7.2km) south-west of Modbury

Dog friendly
On lead in farmland and coastal fields; precipitous unfenced cliffs

OS maps
Landranger 202 (Torbay & South Dartmoor), Explorer OL20 (South Devon)

GPS waypoints
SX 635 478
Ⓐ SX 632 480
Ⓑ SX 620 478
Ⓒ SX 614 465
Ⓓ SX 635 458
Ⓔ SX 637 475

Kingston and the River Erme

This tucked-away corner of the county is relatively little visited even in the height of summer, and worth a lengthy drive along narrow high-hedged lanes. The route visits the beautiful Erme estuary then turns east along a stunning stretch of rugged coastline, culminating in a steep and sometimes slippery descent to Westcombe Beach.

Kingston The pretty and historic village of Kingston – King Aethulwulf, father of Alfred the Great, acquired land here in AD876 – gives no indication of its proximity to one of South Devon's loveliest rivers and most impressive (and quietest) coastal landscapes. This is a walk that starts gently and builds up both in terms of difficulty and grandeur: an easy stroll along the peaceful Erme river – the land on the opposite bank is part of the Flete Estate, recorded in the Domesday Book – leads to some of South Devon's most dramatic coastal landscapes.

The walk starts from the 14th-century parish church. With the church on your left follow the lane uphill to Wonwell Gate and turn right along the lane. After bends turn left Ⓐ through a gate signed to Wonwell Beach.

Keep along the left edge of the field: at a hedge corner bear right across the field to a stile onto an enclosed path. Pass a stile and keep along the left edge of two fields, via a stile, with

The Dolphin Inn sits in the heart of Kingston

Map labels:

River, Skerrit, Coppice, Quarry Garden Plantation, Torr Down, Blackpost Cross, Cocks Park, Watton Park, Great Torr, Four Torr Cross, 113, Boult Hill Plantation, Boat Hill Copse, 48, 119, A, Vicarage Farm, 17, Torr Farm, Old Coastguard Cottages, B, 12, Furzedown Wood, Cross (restored), P.Sta., Kingston, BS, Wrinkle Wood, Wonwell Court Farm, KINGSTON CP, E, Limekiln (disused), 62, 63, 119, 64, Malthouse Point, 47, Okenbury, 101, Wonwell Beach, 108, RIN, Muxham Point, Scobbiscombe Farm, 98, 114, Wiscombe Lane, Fernycombe Beach, 106, 114, The Beacon, Broad Cliff Copse, South West Coast Path, Freshwater, 100, 90, Hoist Point, 46, 101, Low, Beacon Beach, Hoist Beach, Beacon Point, Guttersлide Beach, Westcombe Beach, Meddrick Rocks, Ayrmer Cove, Toby's Point

SCALE 1:25000 or 2½ INCHES to 1 MILE 4CM to 1KM

0 200 400 600 800 METRES 1 KILOMETRES
0 200 400 600 YARDS ½ MILES

views to the southern slopes of Dartmoor. Cross a stile into woodland (carpeted with bluebells in May), soon descending steeply to reach the lane to Wonwell Beach **B** and turn left.

At the top of Wonwell Slipway (where Coast Path walkers must wade across the river at low tide) bear left on the Coast Path, which runs through woodland and then along the back of Wonwell Beach (where lie the remains of the pilot's cottage: when the river was navigable a pilot was required to guide incoming cargo boats over the sand bars).

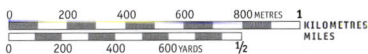

The Coast Path hugs low cliffs towards Fernycombe Point – listen out for the cries of oystercatchers on the beach below, look back for views upriver to Dartmoor and across the river mouth to Meadowsfoot Beach and the coastguard cottages on the historic Flete Estate – then passes through a stile onto National Trust land at Scobbiscombe Farm **C**.

From this point on the cliffs increase in height and the route becomes more

Dramatic Cliffs, Hoist Point

taxing. Follow the cliff edge to round The Beacon, then keep along a fence inland from the cliffs. The path hugs the cliffs again above Gutterslide Beach, before descending into and out of a combe near Broad Cliff Copse. Pass a path to Scobbiscombe, then follow the cliff edge again to gain the top of Hoist Point, with glorious views east to Burgh Island and its Art Deco hotel.

From here the Coast Path zigzags very steeply downhill – be aware that after wet weather the path may be slippery, and that the cliffs here are sheer – to run along the back of Westcombe Beach.

Turn left **D** at a sign to Kingston along a fenced path, soon crossing a footbridge. The path winds through woodland to a stile. Keep ahead where a bridleway bears off left, and continue along a hedged path to pass a lake (right). Cross a farm track and keep straight on, climbing gently past more lakes and entering woodland: stretches of this track are often muddy.

At a path junction **E** keep ahead on a rough track that soon becomes tarmac, uphill, past houses. By Rock Cottage turn right downhill, then first left to pass the 16th-century **Dolphin Inn** and return to your car. ●

Bolt Head and Salcombe Estuary

Start

North Sands car park at south end of Salcombe town

Distance

6 miles (9.4km)

Height gain

920 feet (280m)

Approximate time

3½ hours

Route terrain

Country lanes and fields, undulating Coast Path, parts very rocky underfoot; steep climb towards finish

Parking

North Sands (pay & display)

Dog friendly

On lead through Higher Soar

OS maps

Landranger 202 (Torbay & South Dartmoor), Explorer OL20 (South Devon)

GPS waypoints

SX 730 382
Ⓐ SX 729 379
Ⓑ SX 713 382
Ⓒ SX 711 379
Ⓓ SX 707 377
Ⓔ SX 706 369
Ⓕ SX 722 363
Ⓖ SX 729 374

Initially this is an undulating inland walk, involving several climbs which bring you to the coast. There then follows a superb stretch of coastal walking to the prominent headland of Bolt Head at the mouth of the Salcombe estuary. The final part of the walk is the most spectacular and energetic, as you proceed around the headland, across the sheer face of Sharp Tor, before descending gently through attractive woodland along the western side of the estuary. On this last stretch there are fine views ahead of Salcombe Harbour.

The walk begins by the beach at North Sands at the southern end of the attractive resort, fishing port and sailing centre of Salcombe. Guarding the entrance to the harbour are the sparse remains of a 16th-century artillery fort built by Henry VIII.

Turn right out of the car park, follow the road uphill, first around a right bend and then a sharp left bend, and at the top, just before the lane drops towards South Sands, turn right Ⓐ along an uphill lane. At a fork continue along the left-hand lane (Moult Road). This shortly becomes a rough track. Keep

Sharp Tor seen from Bolt Head, at the mouth of the estuary

ahead at a footpath fork and climb steadily to enter an area of woodland, by a public footpath sign. Keep ahead along a narrow path and climb a stile, after which the path descends and continues as an enclosed, hedge-lined path. Emerge on to a lane and continue along it, eventually descending past some attractive thatched cottages.

At a fork take the left-hand lane, signed 'Rew' and 'Malborough'. The lane drops then climbs steadily. After 1/4 mile turn left along a tarmac drive **B**, at a public footpath sign to Soar, passing Higher Rew Farm. Keep ahead as signed along a hedge-lined path, by a caravan and camping site on the left. This path curves left and enters a field. Turn right and head uphill along the right edge to join a field-edge track. Bear left along this and eventually turn right by a cattle-grid to a meeting of lanes and tracks **C**. Keep straight ahead along the lane to a junction in front of a holiday home development. Turn left along a lane to Soar Mill Cove, and head downhill to a public footpath sign in front of a thatched cottage **D**.

Turn left to pass in front of the cottage, cross a stream and keep along an enclosed path to pass through a gate. Keep ahead, soon following the path right. Pass through a gate then bear

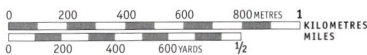

SCALE 1:25 000 or 2½ INCHES to 1 MILE 4CM to 1KM

The Coast Path towards rocky Sharp Tor

slightly left across a field and then head uphill between gorse bushes to a stile at the top edge of the field. Climb it and continue along the right edge of several fields, by a hedge on the right, and over a succession of stiles. After a kissing-gate – by a fingerpost – keep ahead to pass through a gate onto the clifftop where you reach the Coast Path **E**.

Turn left and follow the path along a rugged and most attractive stretch of the coast following signs for Bolt Head and Salcombe. Eventually pass through a gate. Keep ahead to pass another post, then drop to go through a small gate, and follow the Coast Path as it climbs on to Bolt Head. On all sides the views along this spectacular and rocky coastline are quite superb.

Follow the clifftop round to the left; go through a gate at a path junction **F** then follow the Coast Path right

downhill into a hollow with a crag to the right. The path bears left along the edge of the cliff above Starehole Bay and descends into Starehole Bottom, crossing a stream. Go through a gate and continue steadily uphill, via steps, to follow the contours around the sheer face of Sharp Tor. After rounding the tor, descend some steps to continue above the estuary with a succession of attractive views of Salcombe Harbour.

Later the path continues through beautiful coastal woods, goes through a kissing-gate and later through another gate, and eventually meets a lane **G**. Keep going ahead (downhill), bending first to the left and then sharply to the right to pass the **South Sands** and **Tides Reach** hotels. Follow the lane steeply uphill then down to return to North Sands and the **Winking Prawn Café** by the car park. ●

Start Point and Hallsands

From the prominent headland of Start Point the views along the coast in both directions are outstanding and extensive: northwards across the wide expanse of Start Bay to Berry Head near Brixham, and westwards along one of the most spectacular stretches of the South Devon coast to Prawle Point and beyond to Bolt Head near Salcombe. After a short walk to Start Point, the route continues by heading westwards along the often rocky and dramatic Coast Path to Lannacombe Beach, and then turns inland through a steep-sided, wooded valley. An undulating section along lanes, steep in places, brings you back to the coast at the abandoned fishing village of Hallsands and the final stretch is a steady climb of nearly 1 mile above Start Bay. This is a superb walk but there are narrow paths in places and some fairly energetic climbs.

Begin by going through a white gate and walking along the tarmac lighthouse road to Start Point. At a fingerpost **A** keep ahead along the road for a short detour to the lighthouse at the tip of Start Point **B** to enjoy the magnificent views that encompass a large stretch of the South Devon coast.

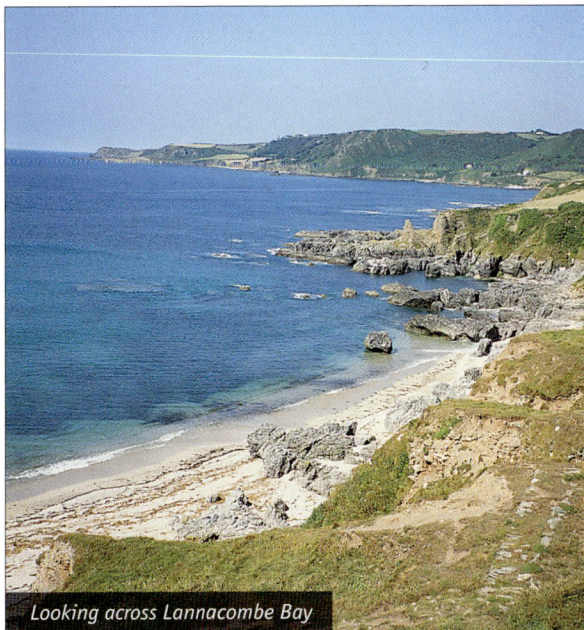
Looking across Lannacombe Bay

walk 19

Start
Start Point

Distance
6½ miles (10.4km)

Height gain
935 feet (285m)

Approximate time
3½ hours

Route terrain
Undulating Coast Path, rocky in places; several steady climbs

Parking
Car park (fee-paying) at Start Point, 3½ miles (5.6km) south of Stokenham

Dog friendly
On lead on Coast Path: sheer unfenced sections

OS maps
Landranger 202 (Torbay & South Dartmoor), Explorer OL20 (South Devon)

GPS waypoints
 SX 820 375
A SX 824 372
B SX 829 371
C SX 802 372
D SX 803 383
E SX 817 385

Start Point from the Coast Path north of Hallsands

Return to the fingerpost and turn left **A** along the Coast Path which cuts across the narrow neck of the point. The path makes initially for Frenchman's Rock, passing around the jagged pinnacles – *take care here, there are some sheer drops*. On the next part of the walk the views across Lannacombe Bay to Prawle Point are outstanding as you follow the winding and undulating path along this dramatic and rugged coast to reach Lannacombe Beach.

Go through a gate just before reaching the beach and turn right **C**, leaving the Coast Path, and continue along a narrow, tree- and hedge-lined track – later it becomes a tarmac track – for 1 mile through a thickly wooded and steep-sided valley.

At a T-junction, turn right **D** to continue along a lane which heads uphill to a crossroads at Hollowcombe Head. Keep ahead, in the South Hallsands direction, and the lane soon turns right and descends to the coast above the ruined fishing village of

Hallsands (which can be seen from the viewing platform – follow the signs). Turn right **E** on to the Coast Path for a steady, continuous climb of 1 mile to return to the start, enjoying more fine views of Start Point and Start Bay. ●

Hallsands The village was abandoned after being destroyed during a violent storm in January 1917 and controversy has raged ever since over why this disaster was actually allowed to happen and was not avoided. One theory blames the sand dredging operations, which had been allowed since 1897, alleging that these had lowered the level of the beach, which used to protect the village. But over the centuries other villages on this stretch of coast have been similarly destroyed by the sea, so perhaps the catastrophe was inevitable.

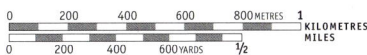

SCALE 1:25000 or 2½ INCHES to 1 MILE *4CM to 1KM*

0   200   400   600   800 METRES   1
KILOMETRES
MILES
0   200   400   600 YARDS   ½

Torcross, Slapton Ley and Stokenham

Start
Torcross

Distance
7 miles (11.2km)

Height gain
755 feet (230m)

Approximate time
3½ hours

Route terrain
Narrow ley-side paths, quiet lanes, fields, Coast Path; steady ascent from C

P Parking
Car park on north side of village (pay & display), 6½ miles (10.5km) east of Kingsbridge

Dog friendly
On lead in nature reserve and farmland

OS maps
Landranger 202 (Torbay & South Dartmoor), Explorer OL20 (South Devon)

GPS waypoints
SX 823 424
A SX 827 443
B SX 821 443
C SX 813 445
D SX 802 434
E SX 806 432
F SX 807 427
G SX 820 413

There is a great variety of terrain and considerable historic interest on this walk. The scenic variety includes a walk beside the raised shingle beach of Slapton Sands, the lagoon and marshlands of Slapton Ley Nature Reserve, some pleasant woodland and a stretch along the Coast Path. On the final descent into Torcross a superb view unfolds along the length of Start Bay, with the whole of the route spread out before you. Historic interest ranges from the medieval church at Stokenham to a hitherto largely unknown Second World War disaster, commemorated by the tank at the start of the walk. The first 2½ miles are fairly flat; after that be prepared for several lengthy and fairly steep climbs.

Wartime tragedy

The black Sherman tank at the south end of the car park was recovered from the seabed in 1984 and placed here as a memorial to over 900 US servicemen, killed by a surprise German attack in April 1944 while rehearsing for the D-Day landings. News of the tragedy was suppressed at the time and for many years it remained largely unknown until a local man, Ken Small, wrote a book about it and played a major role in organising the tank memorial.

At the north end of the car park a path leads off through a gate and runs parallel to, and just below, the road across the narrow causeway between the sea and the freshwater lagoon of Slapton Ley. After 1¼ miles the path reaches a lane. Turn left along this and after crossing Slapton Bridge turn left A through a gate, at a public footpath sign, to follow a path through Slapton Ley National Nature Reserve, an important habitat for wildfowl. The path, attractively tree-lined in places, keeps by the water and proceeds up and down steps, over stiles and across boardwalks. After bearing right along the right edge of a marshy area, you reach a fingerpost in front of a gate. Turn left B, in the 'Permissive Route, Slapton Village' direction. Continue across more boardwalks, bending left along the left edge of the marsh to another fingerpost. Keep ahead, in the 'Deer Bridge' direction, along a tree-lined path to emerge on to a lane C.

Turn
left over
Deer Bridge
and follow the
lane steadily
uphill for 1 mile,
curving gradually left
to reach a junction of
lanes at Coleridge Cross.
At a public footpath sign **D**
bear to the left, then head
diagonally right across a field, aiming
for a tall footpath post. Go through a
gate and continue straight across the
next field to go through a gate on to a
lane **E**. Turn right downhill into
Stokenham, an attractive village of
whitewashed cottages, some of which
are thatched, and presided over by an
unusually large and imposing
15th-century church – a fine example
of the Perpendicular style. Like other
villages in the area, Stokenham was
evacuated in 1943 so that American
troops could use it while making
preparations for D-Day.

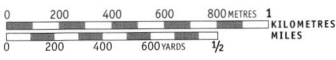

At a T-junction, turn right and almost
immediately turn sharp left down a
narrow, enclosed lane to another
T-junction. Turn left (**Tradesmans Arms**
right) and follow the lane as it bends

SCALE 1:27777 or about 2¼ INCHES to 1 MILE 3.6CM to 1KM

							METRES	1	
0	200	400	600	800			KILOMETRES		
							MILES		
0	200	400	600	YARDS	½				

Slapton Ley from Slapton Bridge

right to pass the church (**Church House Inn** right) to meet the main road **F**. Cross over, take the narrow, uphill lane opposite to a T-junction. Keep ahead through a metal kissing-gate, at a public footpath sign to Beeson, and continue uphill across a field towards a lone sycamore. Near the top keep by a wire fence on the right to go through another metal kissing-gate and continue to a tarmac track. Turn left along this through woodland. Opposite gates the track bears left and continues (signed 'Public Footpath') down to a thatched cottage. Follow a path to the left of the cottage and continue gently downhill along the left inside edge of woodland to a stile. Climb this, cross a track, climb another stile opposite and bear to the left to keep alongside the right edge of a sloping field.

Towards the field corner climb a stile on the right and continue down an enclosed path to reach a T-junction **G**. Turn left to join the Coast Path, heading uphill through woodland, and follow this as it curves right, around the rim of Beesands Quarry, before descending to a gate. Go through the gate to emerge from the trees and continue downhill along a grassy path to another gate. From this path the view right to Beesands and Start Point, and later ahead over Start Bay, Slapton Sands and Slapton Ley is magnificent, and almost the whole route of the walk can be seen.

Go through the next gate and continue downhill along an enclosed path which eventually bends sharp right down to a tarmac track. Follow the track round a left bend and, at a waymarked post, turn sharp right. Walk along a gravel track, passing in front of houses, until this narrows to a path and descends steps to the promenade at Torcross. Continue along here, passing the **Seabreeze café** and **Start Bay Inn**, eventually turning left to reach the car park. ●

Beer and Branscombe

This is a highly attractive and varied walk that includes two idyllic villages, a picturesque old church, beautiful woodland, impressive cliffs and coastal views that extend from Lyme Bay to Torbay. From Beer the route heads inland along tracks and field paths to Branscombe. The shorter version proceeds directly to the coast but the full walk continues to Branscombe church and on through lovely coastal woodlands before descending steeply to the beach at Branscombe Mouth. The final stretch of the walk takes the 'Undercliff' route, a narrow and winding path through a landslip below the chalk face of Beer Head, before climbing to the clifftop and continuing back to Beer.

> **Beer**
> Beer is an exceptionally attractive village, with a sheltered location below the chalk cliffs of Beer Head, stone cottages, a small stream flowing down the main street to the sea and fishing boats drawn up on to the pebble beach. As well as being a fishing village – with incomes occasionally supplemented by smuggling – Beer was, in the past, also renowned for the local freestone, worked since Roman times and used in buildings all over the country. The underground caverns of Beer Quarry Caves – once a hiding place for smuggled goods – are well worth a visit.

🔖 The walk starts at the bottom end of Cliff Top car park. Follow the Coast Path down the 'No Entry' road (Common Lane) which descends steeply into Beer and turn left up Fore Street to walk through the village, passing to the left of the Victorian church, bearing left along The Causeway Ⓐ. Keep ahead at the

The Mason's Arms at Branscombe

---

walk 21

🔖 Start
Beer, Cliff Top car park

Distance
6¼ miles (9.9km), shorter version 4¾ miles (7.6km)

Height gain
1,180 feet (360m), shorter version 870 feet (265m)

⏱ Approximate time
3½ hours, shorter version 2½ hours

Route terrain
Field paths, woodland tracks, Coast Path uneven underfoot in places; steady ascents from Ⓐ and Ⓔ

Ⓟ Parking
Beer Cliff Top car park (pay & display), 2½ miles (4km) south-west of Seaton

Dog friendly
On lead in farmland

OS maps
Landranger 192 (Exeter & Sidmouth), Explorers 116 (Lyme Regis & Bridport) and 115 (Exmouth & Sidmouth)

GPS waypoints
🔖 SY 228 888
Ⓐ SY 228 894
Ⓑ SY 224 892
Ⓒ SY 211 890
Ⓓ SY 204 886
Ⓔ SY 195 884
Ⓕ SY 196 882
Ⓖ SY 207 881

---

next junction, in the Branscombe direction, and turn left along Mare Lane. Head uphill, go round a right-hand bend and where the road bears slightly left towards Beer Head, turn right **B**, still along Mare Lane, and continue up to pass to the right of Pecorama (gardens and railway).

Take the tarmac, hedge-lined track to the left of the car park entrance. This shortly becomes a rough track – still Mare Lane – which you follow for just under 1 mile, passing into fields en route, to a T-junction of tracks **C**. Keep ahead through a kissing-gate. Walk across a field and go through a kissing-gate on the far side. Turn right along the right edge of the next field, and almost immediately left to follow the field edge. Turn right over a stile in the field corner. Bear right along a downhill path through attractive woodland, curving left at a public footpath sign to Branscombe. Continue downhill, ignoring a path right, to a stile. Climb this and continue steeply downhill along an enclosed path – there are fine views from here of Branscombe village and church – to a lane and turn left.

After a few yards at the lane junction the full walk turns right **D** *(at this point the shorter version turns left along the lane to rejoin the full walk at Branscombe Mouth* **G***)* along a lane which heads down into the very attractive and rather scattered village of Branscombe. The main part, called Vicarage, is a picturesque collection of cottages grouped around the pub. Another group of cottages lies near the church over ½ mile away. At a T-junction, turn left, in the Sidmouth direction, passing **The Masons Arms** Hotel on the right. Continue along the lane, passing a thatched working smithy (opposite **The Old Bakery Tearooms**) up to the cruciform church, one of the

Branscombe Mouth

loveliest village churches in Devon with a fine Norman tower.

Pass through the gate into the churchyard **E**. Keep ahead past the east end of the church, then drop downhill across the grass between two big cedar trees, to a stile. Climb this, keep ahead to cross a footbridge over a stream, head steeply uphill along the right edge of a meadow and climb a stile in the corner to enter woodland. Follow a winding path up steps and climb a stile. Turn left, still heading uphill through woodland, to reach a T-junction **F**. Turn left along the Coast Path, which you follow for the

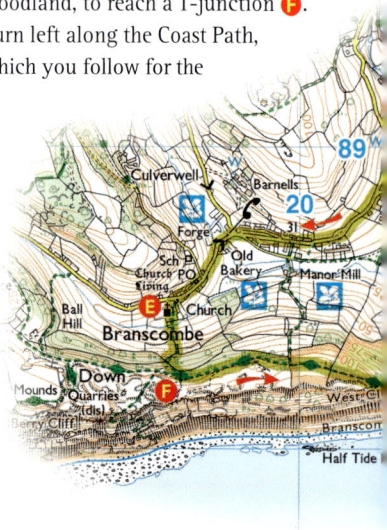

remainder of the route. The next stage of the walk is particularly attractive as you continue through woodland, passing through several gates and with attractive views over Branscombe and the valley to the left.

Eventually you emerge from the trees to descend steeply, via steps in places. Pass through a gate and continue downhill. Turn right through an open gateway and continue ahead to reach Branscombe Mouth 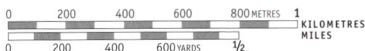. Turn left on the Coast Path to pass the **Sea Shanty**. It is difficult to believe that this pretty thatched tearoom above the beach was once a coal yard, importing coal from South Wales. Cross a stream, turn right through a kissing-gate and head uphill to a fingerpost. Keep ahead through a gate, in the 'Coast Path, Beer' direction, and walk along a track through a small static caravan site below East Cliff. This is the 'Undercliff' route. Look out for a 'Coast Path' sign which directs you to the right off the track to continue along

a narrow, undulating path that twists and turns through the landslip below the cliff. The going is quite difficult in places but eventually the path zigzags up steps to the top of Beer Head, 130m (426ft) high and the most westerly of the chalk headlands on the south coast of England.

> **Beer Head** From here you can enjoy superlative views along the coast almost from Portland Bill on the Dorset coast to Berry Head on the far side of Torbay.

At the top go through a kissing-gate and turn right to follow the Coast Path around Beer Head, negotiating several gates, and enjoying more superb views as you continue towards Beer. Above Beer beach bear to the left, keeping by a hedge on the left, towards a caravan site and Cliff Top car park. After passing through a kissing-gate, continue along an enclosed path which bends right and eventually passes the car park to emerge on to the road at the starting point. ●

SCALE 1:25 000 or 2½ INCHES to 1 MILE 4CM to 1KM

🗸 Start

Cold East Cross
(junction of roads to
Newton Abbot,
Ponsworthy, Ashburton
and Widecombe in
the Moor)

🗸 Distance

6½ miles (10.3km),
shorter version
5½ miles (8.8km)

🗸 Height gain

1,035 feet (315m),
shorter version
820 feet (250m)

🗸 Approximate time

3½ hours, shorter
version 3 hours

🗸 Route terrain

Moorland paths and
woodland tracks,
sometimes boggy and
rough; steady descent/
ascent to/from **F**

🅿 Parking

Cold East Cross (free),
4 miles (6.4km) south-
west of Haytor Vale

🗸 Dog friendly

Under control at all
times; on lead in
nesting season
(1 March–15 July)

🗸 OS maps

Landranger 191
(Okehampton & North
Dartmoor), Explorer
OL28 (Dartmoor)

🗸 GPS waypoints

🗸 SX 740 742
A SX 746 755
B SX 736 762
C SX 732 757
D SX 727 744
E SX 724 738
F SX 720 731
G SX 735 731

Rippon Tor, Pil Tor and Buckland Beacon

*Apart from the initial climb to Rippon Tor, this walk offers
dramatic and ever-changing views over Dartmoor for relatively
little effort. This is very much a 'tor-bagging' route that takes in
Rippon Tor, Top Tor, Pil Tor, Tunhill Rocks and last, but not
least, Buckland Beacon which is a particularly outstanding
viewpoint. The full walk includes a ¾ mile (1.2km) diversion to
the attractive hamlet of Buckland in the Moor.*

⚠ Without the tors to act as guides, this would be a difficult
walk to follow in misty weather and should not be attempted
in such conditions unless you are able to navigate using a
compass.

🗸 Begin by walking north along the road, in the Haytor
and Widecombe in the Moor direction. After ¼ mile where the
wall on the right bends to the right, turn right, and, almost
immediately, turn left uphill across the open moor. On joining a
wall on the right keep beside it to reach the first group of rocks,
the Nut Crackers. Continue uphill, go through a gate and bear
left up to Rippon Tor **A**, 1,552ft (473m) the first of a series of
superb viewpoints on this walk. The views extend over a large
area of Dartmoor, to the Teign estuary and to the coast.

Looking west from the tor, take the obvious path towards the
bottom right-hand corner of the down below, just before a road
junction. Pass through a small gate in the wall at the bottom,

Haytor Rocks, seen from the summit of Rippon Tor

then ahead through a gate by the cattle-grid to reach Hemsworthy Gate. Cross the Ashburton road, keep ahead across a small parking area and follow a path that heads up to Top Tor **B**. From here turn left and make your way across to the more impressive Pil Tor. Bear right to pass through the middle of the rocks and follow a path, gently downhill to the next group, Tunhill Rocks. All the way the views are glorious, especially over the Webburn valley to the right where Widecombe in the Moor church tower is a prominent landmark.

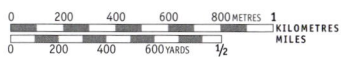

At Tunhill Rocks turn left **C**, head downhill to a wall corner and continue alongside a wall on the right to a ladder-stile. Climb this, continue along the right edge of moorland, still by a wall on the right, and just before reaching a gate and a corner, bear left to climb another ladder-stile and turn right down to a lane. Turn left, immediately follow the lane around a right-hand bend and, where it bears

SCALE 1:27777 or about 2¼ INCHES to 1 MILE 3.6CM to 1KM

Looking towards Widecombe church from Tunhill Rocks

slightly left, keep straight ahead along a path across Pudsham Down, by a hedgebank on the right. After the hedgebank turns right keep ahead, between gorse, bracken and heather, to a road **D**. Cross over, go through a gate, at a public bridleway sign, and continue ahead downhill along the attractive, hedge- and partially tree-lined track ahead – it later becomes a tarmac track.

After nearly ½ mile another tarmac track leads off to the left **E**. *Turn left along it if you wish to omit the detour to Buckland in the Moor.* Otherwise keep ahead, descending more steeply, to emerge on to a road opposite St Peter's Church **F**. The picturesque hamlet of Buckland – a group of thatched cottages nestling below the steep, wooded slopes of Buckland Beacon – sits further down the road below the church.

Retrace your steps to **E** and turn right along the tarmac track. The track descends to Bowden Farm. Opposite the farm entrance bear left through a metal gate on a public bridle-path. The rough track crosses a stream, ascends along the left edge of a plantation and

continues between walls to pass through a gate onto moorland. Keep ahead for a few yards, then soon turn right, meeting a wall right; soon bear left (before reaching an area of gorse) to pick your way uphill across rough ground to gain Buckland Beacon **G**. At 1,250ft (381m), this is another magnificent viewpoint looking over the thickly wooded and steep-sided Holne Chase and Dart gorge, with open moorland on the horizon and Buckland in the Moor church immediately below. Two granite stones here were carved with the Ten Commandments in 1928 by the same man who arranged for 'My Dear Mother' to be inscribed on the clock face of Buckland church instead of the usual numerals.

With your back to the view, take the path which keeps alongside a wall on the right. Where the wall curves right keep ahead uphill on a grassy path, aiming for Rippon Tor which will be seen ahead and following a line of widely spaced boundary markers. Eventually bear right to drop to Cold East Cross. ●

Widgery Cross and Great Links Tor

walk 23

Start
Car park north-east of Dartmoor Inn off A386

Distance
6½ miles (10.5km)

Height gain
1,130 feet (345m)

Approximate time
3½ hours

Route terrain
Moorland tracks and paths, some indistinct and rough underfoot; steady ascent from Ⓐ to Ⓑ

P Parking
Car park (free) ¼ mile (400m) along lane leading north-east from Dartmoor Inn, Lydford

Dog friendly
Under control at all times; on lead in nesting season (1 March–15 July)

OS maps
Landranger 191 (Okehampton & North Dartmoor), Explorer OL28 (Dartmoor)

GPS waypoints
- SX 525 853
- Ⓐ SX 530 857
- Ⓑ SX 539 855
- Ⓒ SX 551 861
- Ⓓ SX 550 867
- Ⓔ SX 552 871
- Ⓕ SX 545 887
- Ⓖ SX 530 863

Two tors are climbed on this walk: the first ascent, to Widgery Cross on the summit of Brat Tor 1,482 feet (452m), is steep; the second, to the impressive bulk of Great Links Tor 1,922 feet (586m), is relatively easy. After descending from Great Links Tor, the route is along clear and well-defined tracks, mostly using disused railway lines that used to serve a peat works. The entire walk is across open moorland on the western edge of Dartmoor and the views are both tremendous and extensive, especially westwards towards Cornwall and Bodmin Moor.

⚠ There is some rough walking and you are advised not to attempt this in bad weather or misty conditions unless you are an experienced walker able to navigate using a compass.

🖊 Start by walking along the grassy track that leads out of the top left corner of the car park and runs roughly parallel to the vehicle track on the left. Immediately there is a fine view of both the tors that are to be climbed: Brat Tor, which is crowned by Widgery Cross, slightly to the right and Great Links Tor ahead. Continue along the track which descends fairly gently before joining the vehicle track Ⓐ near a ford, footbridge and stepping stones across the River Lyd. This is a delightful spot.

Cross the river and bear half-right off the track to continue along a clear, grassy path heading steeply up to the summit of Brat Tor Ⓑ. This is quite a strenuous climb but the view from the top, over Dartmoor and West Devon, is superb. Immediately below are Lydford Castle and church. Widgery Cross was erected in 1887 to commemorate Queen Victoria's Golden Jubilee.

At the summit face due east and bear half-left to head across grassy moorland in the direction of the prominent bulk of Great Links Tor on the skyline. On meeting a sunken track, turn right and follow this rocky, grassy old tin miners' track until you

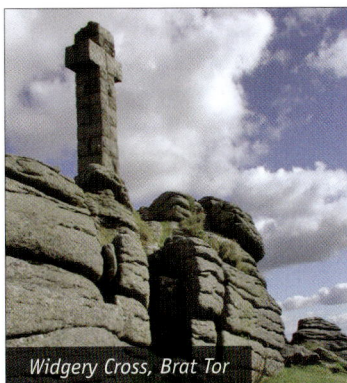
Widgery Cross, Brat Tor

The view west from Great Nodden

reach a boundary stone on the left, roughly where the embankments lining the track peter out. At the stone, turn left **C** and continue gently uphill across the rough, open moor to the triangulation pillar on Great Links Tor **D**, a most impressive collection of rocks and another magnificent viewpoint over the area.

Keep on in roughly the same direction, descending across rough and uneven terrain towards the clear track ahead. This is a disused railway track built in 1879 to transport peat from the Rattlebrook Peat Works beyond Great Links Tor. It closed down in 1955. Turn left **E** along the track and follow it, as it curves first to the right and later slightly to the left, as far as a junction of tracks **F**. All the way the views to the left across West Devon are superb.

At the junction turn sharp left, almost doubling back, along a track that has been in view below on the left for some time. This clear and well-surfaced track, still part of the old peat line, curves right over the lower slopes of the smooth, rounded hill of Great Nodden, giving more fine views, and descends gently. At a fork take the right-hand track which continues to descend to meet a wall on the right. Where the track curves left, just before reaching the wall corner on the edge of the moor, keep ahead to the corner, Nodden Gate **G**. Turn right through a gate, turn left, and left again through another gate. Turn right, at a public footpath sign, to continue along the right edge of the moor, by a wall on the right. At a fingerpost turn half-left, head gently uphill across grass and over the brow. Descend equally gently, passing a football post, making for a metal gate and

public footpath sign. Climb a stone stile to the right of the gate and turn half-right **A** along a grassy track – not fully right on to the vehicle track – to return to the start.

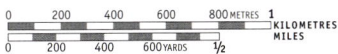

SCALE 1:27777 or about 2¼ INCHES to 1 MILE 3.6CM to 1KM

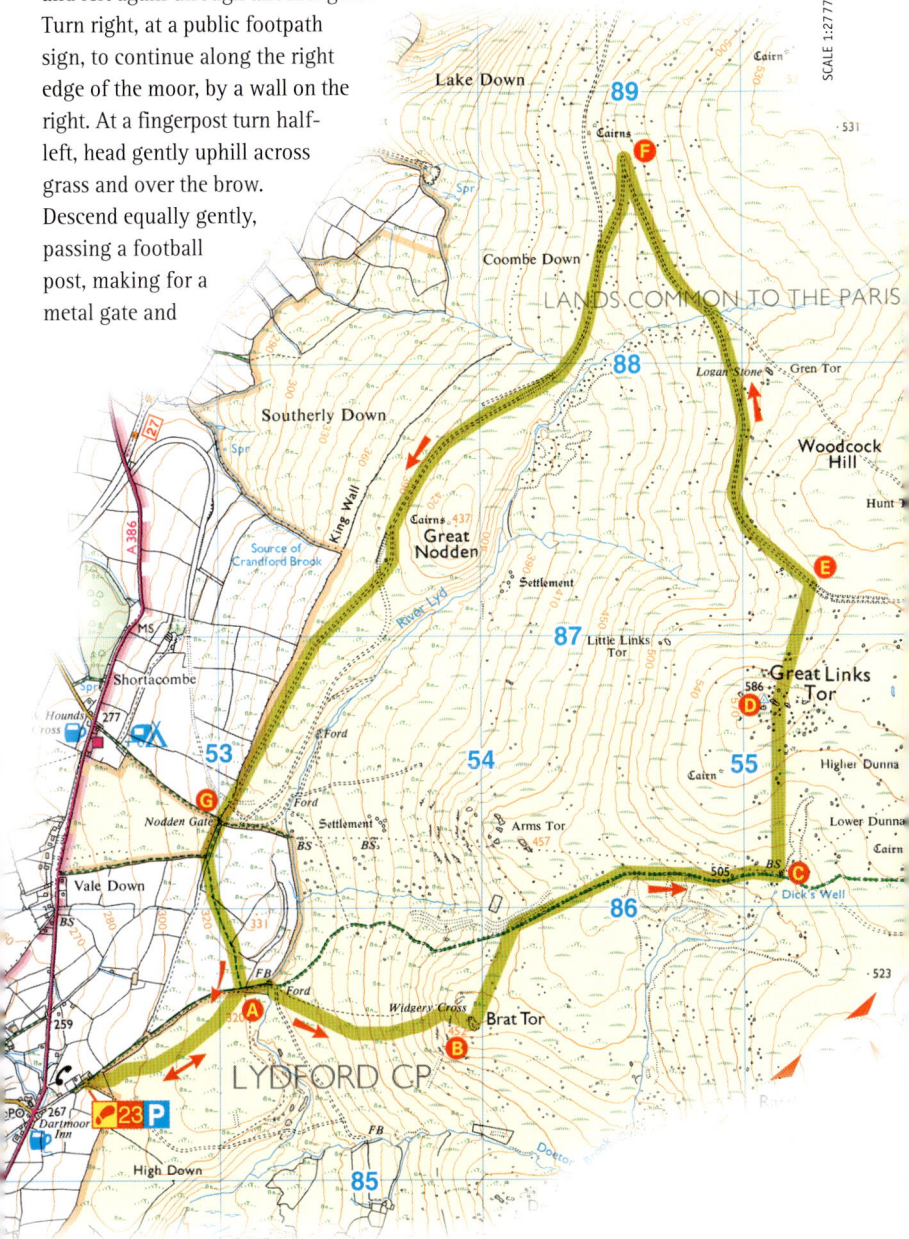

walk 24

Start

Okehampton
Moor Gate

Distance

6¼ miles (9.9km)

Height gain

1,015 feet (310m)

Approximate time

3½ hours

Route terrain

Moorland paths and
tracks

P Parking

Parking area (free) at
Okehampton Moor
Gate, just beyond
Okehampton Camp,
1 mile (1.6km) south
of Okehampton

Dog friendly

Under control at all
times; on lead in
nesting season
(1 March–15 July)

OS maps

Landranger 191
(Okehampton & North
Dartmoor), Explorer
OL28 (Dartmoor)

GPS waypoints

SX 591 931
Ⓐ SX 587 924
Ⓑ SX 582 919
Ⓒ SX 585 908
Ⓓ SX 580 901
Ⓔ SX 580 899
Ⓕ SX 580 892

Yes Tor and High Willhays

Considering that this walk is to the highest points on Dartmoor – and indeed the highest in England south of the Pennines – this is a relatively easy route, mostly on clear tracks and with steady, rather than steep climbs. The only rough moorland walking is the final part of the ascent to Yes Tor 2,030 feet (619m), from where it is an undulating stroll to High Willhays 2,037 feet (621m). The descent could hardly be more straightforward. On good days it is most exhilarating, with glorious views over northern Dartmoor and across mid Devon to the edge of Exmoor.

⚠️ This is not a route to be tackled in bad weather unless you are an experienced walker able to navigate with a compass.

NOTE Part of the walk enters the Okehampton Military Range, which is used for live firing on a limited number of days. The boundaries are marked by red and white posts and by red and white warning noticeboards. Details of firing times can be obtained from National Park information centres or www.dartmoor-ranges.co.uk Do not enter the range at firing times when the red flags are flying, and do not pick up any metal objects while walking within the range area.

Walk down the lane towards Moor Gate. Beyond the cattle grid turn right (do not cross the river) along a tarmac track, above Moor Brook on the left and by a wall bordering the army camp on the right. From the start there is a grand view ahead of West Mill Tor and Yes Tor. Stay on the tarmac track to pass Anthony Stile – a stile and public footpath sign in the wall across grass to the right – and carry on to a junction where the tarmac track turns left Ⓐ. Keep ahead along a rough track that climbs gently over Black Down and at a junction of several tracks, bear left Ⓑ on to a track that you can see heading across grassy moorland and then climbing up to the col between West Mill Tor and Yes Tor.

Follow this track as it winds steadily up and at the col where the track peters out, turn right Ⓒ across rough and boggy grassland towards a path that can be seen leading up to the summit of Yes Tor. Cross a stream (on granite boulders) and continue steeply up to the triangulation pillar Ⓓ.

The path to High Willhays from Yes Tor

Yes Tor This is the second highest point on Dartmoor – and the highest tor – and is a magnificent vantage point with views to the south and east over a large area of Dartmoor, westwards in the direction of Bodmin Moor, and northwards across mid Devon to the distant outline of Exmoor.

High Willhays is straight ahead. Follow a clear and well worn track across a broad ridge; the col **E** is so shallow that it is almost a flat walk. Although it is the highest point on Dartmoor, High Willhays is less impressive than Yes Tor but the views from it are equally outstanding and the summit **F** has a distinct feeling of remoteness.

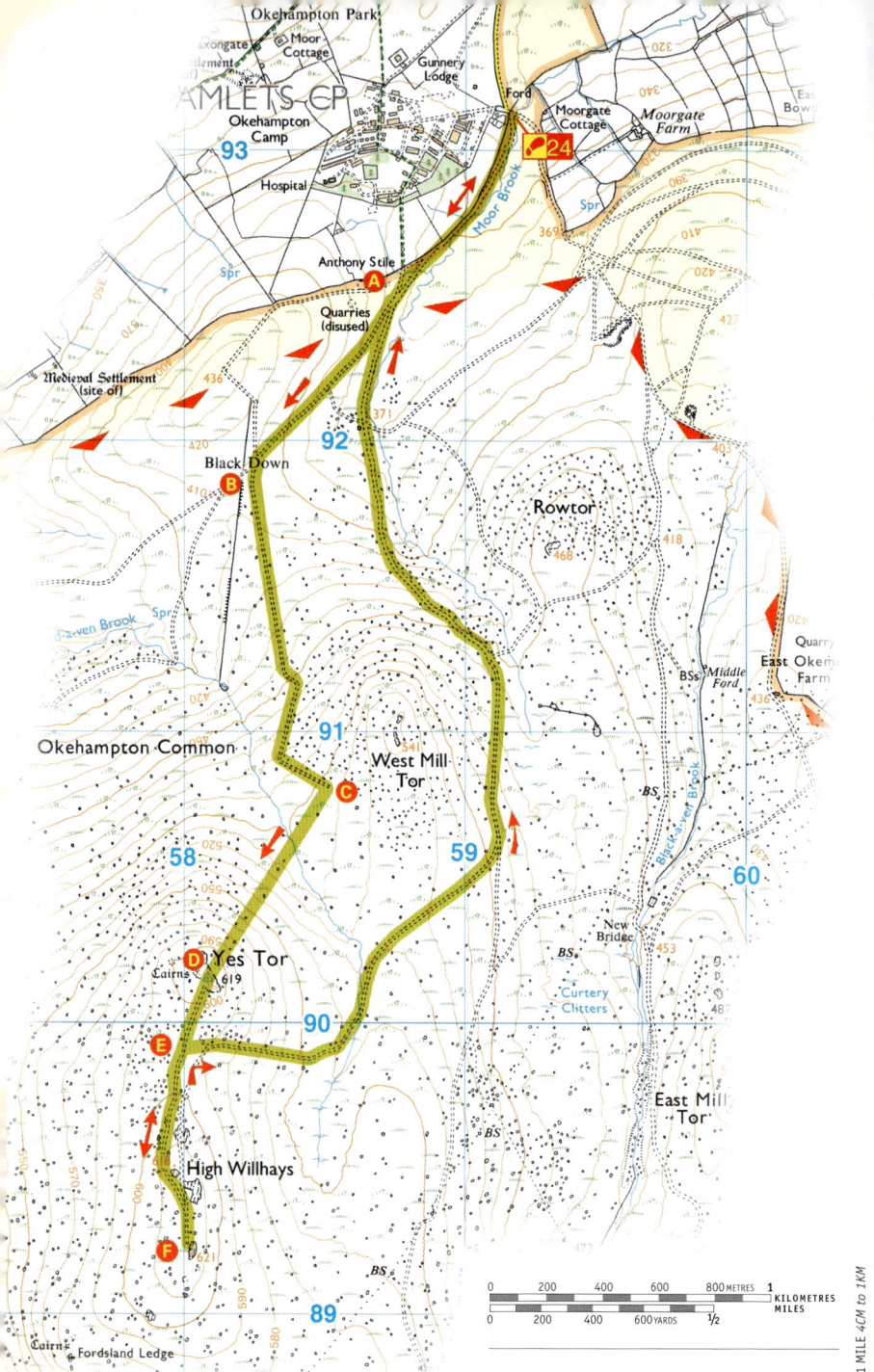

Retrace your steps to the col just below Yes Tor **E** and turn right along a broad, stony track which descends steadily and fairly gently, curving left.

Ford a stream and continue down, at first below Yes Tor and later below West Mill Tor, enjoying more fine views. Keep straight ahead on the main track all the time – later it is tarmac – and follow it back to the start.

SCALE 1:25000 or 2½ INCHES to 1 MILE 4CM to 1KM

Looking east along the beach from Sidmouth

walk 25

Start
Sidmouth

Distance
8 miles (12.8km)

Height gain
1,345 feet (410m)

Approximate time
4 hours

Route terrain
Woodland paths, quiet lanes, strenuous Coast Path: steep ascents/descents

P Parking
Bedford Lawn car park (fee-paying), Station Road, on Sidmouth seafront

Dog friendly
On lead in farmland and Donkey Sanctuary; stretches of precipitous unfenced cliff

OS maps
Landranger 192 (Exeter & Sidmouth), Explorer 115 (Exmouth & Sidmouth)

GPS waypoints
- SY 125 871
- **A** SY 128 878
- **B** SY 129 884
- **C** SY 132 886
- **D** SY 143 885
- **E** SY 151 888
- **F** SY 161 892
- **G** SY 163 880

Sidmouth, Salcombe Regis and Weston Combe

The first part of the walk, a gentle stroll through The Byes beside the little River Sid, is the easiest. This is followed by a long, steady climb over Salcombe Hill to the attractive village of Salcombe Regis. Field paths lead on to the Donkey Sanctuary near the head of Weston Combe, followed by a gentle descent through the beautiful wooded combe to the coast at Weston Mouth. The walk along the Coast Path back to Sidmouth is a strenuous, switchback route of nearly 3 miles over a series of steep and daunting-looking cliffs. Take your time and have frequent rests in order to enjoy the magnificent coastal views on this section of the walk, especially the view over Sidmouth on the final descent of Salcombe Hill Cliff.

Sidmouth

The genteel resort of Sidmouth occupies a sheltered position between steep red sandstone cliffs. It became fashionable during, and just after, the Napoleonic Wars when the English aristocracy were cut off from their usual continental haunts, and the town possesses a number of dignified Georgian and Regency villas, many of them now hotels. Royal prestige was bestowed on the town when the future Queen Victoria stayed here as a young girl with her parents in 1819.

The walk starts on the promenade, built in 1837, at the end of Station Road in front of the **Bedford Hotel**. Facing the beach turn left along the promenade, turn left just past **Hotel Elizabeth** and walk through the pedestrianised town centre; on meeting the High Street keep ahead.

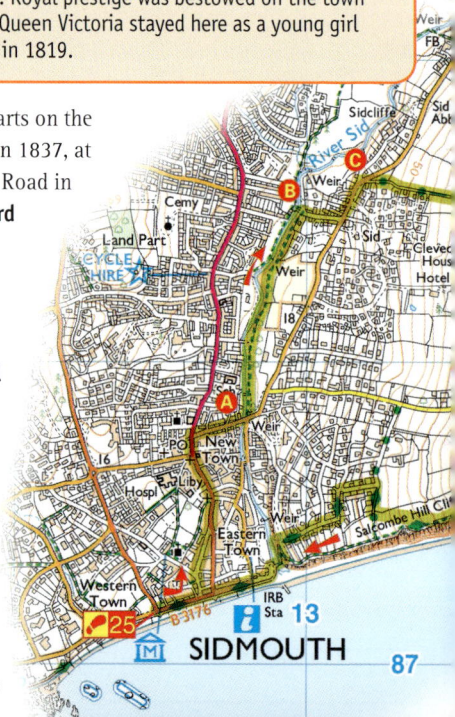

Opposite the Radway Cinema turn right along Salcombe Road; just after crossing the bridge over the River Sid turn left after the old Toll House **A** along a tarmac path that continues through an attractive park beside the river for ½ mile.

At a T-junction, turn right **B** along a lane up to a road, turn left and where the road bears slightly right, bear right **C** up hedged Milltown Lane. Where the lane ends continue uphill, at a 'public bridleway' sign, along an enclosed, tree-lined path. At a fork take the left-hand path and climb a flight of steps to a T-junction of paths and tracks. Turn left along a track heading steadily uphill through attractive woodland. The track bears right to emerge from the trees; keep ahead to eventually go through a gate and onto a road **D**. Turn left, and at a fork by a war memorial, take the right-hand road and continue steeply downhill into Salcombe Regis, a quiet and secluded village of thatched cottages which has an attractive medieval church.

Just past the church turn right along a lane which heads uphill between trees. About 100 yds after emerging from the trees climb a stile on the left **E** at a pubic footpath sign. Walk along the left edge of a field, follow the field edge round to the right, climb a stile and keep ahead across a field to climb another. Continue along the left edge of the next field, climb the stile slightly to the left in the field corner (not the one in the hedge in front) and turn right through a kissing-gate. Keep ahead to pass through another, then two more close together. Continue along an avenue of memorial trees to pass through a kissing-gate on to a lane.

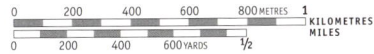

SCALE 1:25 000 or 2½ INCHES to 1 MILE 4CM to 1KM

Turn left and almost immediately right through a gate, following the pedestrian route through the Donkey Sanctuary. This is a home for unwanted and neglected donkeys who are looked after for the rest of their lives and it is open to the public (free entry).

At a public footpath sign to Weston Mouth **F** keep ahead and walk downhill on a narrow path between wooden fences, climbing two stiles at the bottom. Turn right, signed to Weston Mouth, along a path that continues gently downhill through the beautiful, wooded Weston Combe,

negotiating a gate and a stile en route. On meeting a track, bear left and continue downhill, eventually reaching a kissing-gate and a 'Coast Path' sign in the bottom left-hand corner of a meadow. Turn right **G** in the Salcombe Mouth direction, onto the Coast Path.

This is the start of the climb up Lower Dunscombe Cliff. Walk steeply uphill along the left edge of the meadow, following acorn symbols and passing a sign to Weston Plats. Go through the next gate and continue steeply up through trees and along a winding path. Turn sharp left, following the regular

Looking east from Higher Dunscombe Cliff

Looking towards Sidmouth from the Coast Path

Coast Path acorn symbols, to emerge on to the open, grassy clifftop. The view to the east of Weston Cliff is particularly impressive. The path curves inland to a fingerpost, bears left down steps, heads up and bears left again to pass around the deep ravine of Lincombe, later rejoining the top of the cliffs and continuing along to Higher Dunscombe Cliff. Now come superb views looking westwards along the coast to Sidmouth with Torbay on the horizon.

A gate leads to the steep zigzag descent to Salcombe Mouth, stepped in places. Opposite is the daunting sight of Salcombe Hill Cliff. On entering the meadow the official route keeps ahead then turns right above the wooded combe to a fingerpost. Turn left, in the Sidmouth direction, to cross a footbridge over a stream and pass through a kissing-gate. Turn left to keep above Salcombe Mouth.

Now follows one of the most energetic parts of the walk, the steep climb up Salcombe Hill Cliff.

Continue along the clifftop, go through a gate and keep ahead to a viewfinder with a glorious view of Sidmouth before you. Follow the path as it curves right to a path junction by a seat; turn left on the Coast Path and descend steeply via steps through woodland, following acorn symbols ahead all the time. Finally the path crosses a big meadow, descending all the while. At this point the Coast Path has been diverted because of unstable cliffs ahead. Turn right to join an enclosed tarmac path that runs into a narrow lane.

At the end of this turn left down Laskeys Lane between houses. Where the lane bends right, bear left along another tarmac track, and where this ends turn right downhill along a road (Cliff Road). Where the road bends right, keep ahead along a tarmac path which curves left to rejoin the original line of the Coast Path. Bear right and follow the path to cross a bridge over the River Sid. Keep ahead on the promenade to return to the start.

walk 26

Start
Princetown

Distance
10 miles (15.8km)

Height gain
985 feet (300m)

Approximate time
5 hours

Route terrain
Moorland tracks and paths; steady climb from **D** to **E**

Parking
Princetown car park (donations), 8 miles (12.9km) east of Tavistock

Dog friendly
Under control at all times; on lead in nesting season (1 March–15 July)

OS maps
Landrangers 191 (Okehampton & North Dartmoor) and 202 (Torbay & South Dartmoor), Explorer OL28 (Dartmoor)

GPS waypoints
SX 589 735
A SX 565 732
B SX 563 728
C SX 555 715
D SX 560 708
E SX 559 703
F SX 561 695
G SX 574 700
H SX 602 708

Princetown, Dartmoor Railway and Leather Tor

Although this is a long walk amid some of the wildest and emptiest terrain on Dartmoor, most of it is on clear tracks with no rough or strenuous sections, apart from the climb to Sharpitor and Leather Tor, and the subsequent descent to Burrator Reservoir. The area around the reservoir provides some pleasant woodland walking; otherwise the route is entirely across open moorland with extensive and panoramic views, especially from the two tors that are climbed.

⚠️ This walk is, however, in inhospitable country and should not be attempted in bad weather unless you are experienced in such conditions and are able to navigate using a compass. *Save the walk for a fine day when you will be able to savour the high moorland to the full.*

Princetown

'Grim' and 'bleak' are adjectives which are often used to describe Princetown, especially if seen on a grey and misty day. This is partly as a result of its location and surroundings, high up on the open moor, and partly because it is home to Dartmoor's best-known, if least attractive, building – the prison – which appears to match its setting perfectly. Princetown was founded by Sir Thomas Tyrwhitt in the early 19th century and was named after the Prince Regent (later George IV), from whom the land was leased. Tyrwhitt hoped to develop the area into a flourishing agricultural community and to attract people here. It was also he who suggested the building of the prison to house French prisoners from the Napoleonic Wars. The prison was built in 1806 and opened in 1809, closed down at the end of the wars in 1815 and reopened for convicts in 1850. In recent years Princetown has developed into something of a tourist centre with the creation of the High Moorland Visitor Centre which is well worth a visit.

From the car park entrance turn left. Pass the fire station and then bear left on the track signposted 'Disused Railway'. Go through a gate and continue along the track, skirting the edge of a small conifer wood and heading out across open moorland.

Follow the winding track for 1¾ miles, eventually curving right to an intersection of tracks **A**. Turn left along a track that heads gently downhill to join a wall on the left and follow this

Dartmoor railway The railway, which was originally known as the Plymouth and Dartmoor Railway, was built by Sir Thomas Tyrwhitt as a horse-drawn tramway as part of his plan to develop the area around Princetown. It was later converted to a steam-driven railway and mainly transported granite from the local quarries. It was closed down in 1956 and now provides a superb, flat walking and cycling route traversing some of the wildest parts of Dartmoor, with grand views over the countryside in all directions.

wall, to the left, to reach a T-junction of tracks **B**. Turn left here, rejoining the disused railway track, and follow it as it curves first to the right, giving fine views ahead over the Walkham valley, and then to the left around the base of Ingra Tor. Where the track starts to curve right again, turn left off it **C** on to a track that heads uphill. This track later peters out but continue in the same direction to emerge on to a road by a small car park **D**. Cross over and head uphill across rough, trackless moorland, making for the prominent rocky pile of Sharpitor ahead **E**, another magnificent viewpoint.

From here bear to the left and make your way across to Leather Tor, another superb vantage point, especially looking southwards across Burrator Reservoir. Unless you want to climb to the top, walk past the tor, keeping it about 100 yds to your left. Before reaching two outlying rock stacks bear right downhill across rough ground towards the trees and reservoir below. Turn left on reaching a wire fence and wall, and pick your way downhill between rocks, bracken and gorse. Keep the wall on your right to reach a lane by a water channel and a restored cross. Turn left **F** along a track that keeps between the bottom edge of the moor, on the left, and woodland on the right. Bear right to cross a channel. This is the Devonport Leat, which is 15 miles long and was built in the 1790s to bring water from Dartmoor to the naval base at Devonport.

Continue through conifer plantations, keeping on the main track all the while, descending gently and curving right to cross Leather Tor Bridge over the infant River Meavy. Turn left and at a fork a few yards ahead, take the right-hand track which curves right and heads gently uphill, eventually bearing right to a T-junction. Turn left **G** to continue along the right edge of the conifers, between hedge-banks faced with granite blocks. At the corner of the plantation pass between gateposts and continue once more across wild and lonely moorland. Two more crosses can be seen from the track: the first on the

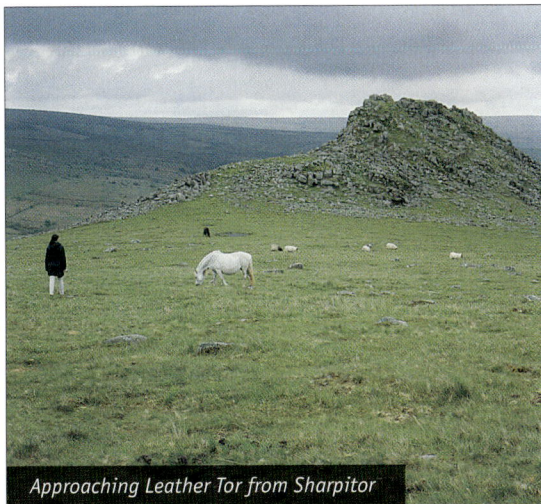

Approaching Leather Tor from Sharpitor

skyline above, the second farther on, to the right. Eventually the track curves right, to cross the Devonport Leat again, then bears left to head up to a crossroads of tracks on top of a low ridge **H**.

Turn left to go along a clear track across the moor back to Princetown, an easy and relaxing finale to the walk. On the horizon directly ahead is the television mast on North Hessary Tor. Later keep by a wall on the right and continue past South Hessary Tor

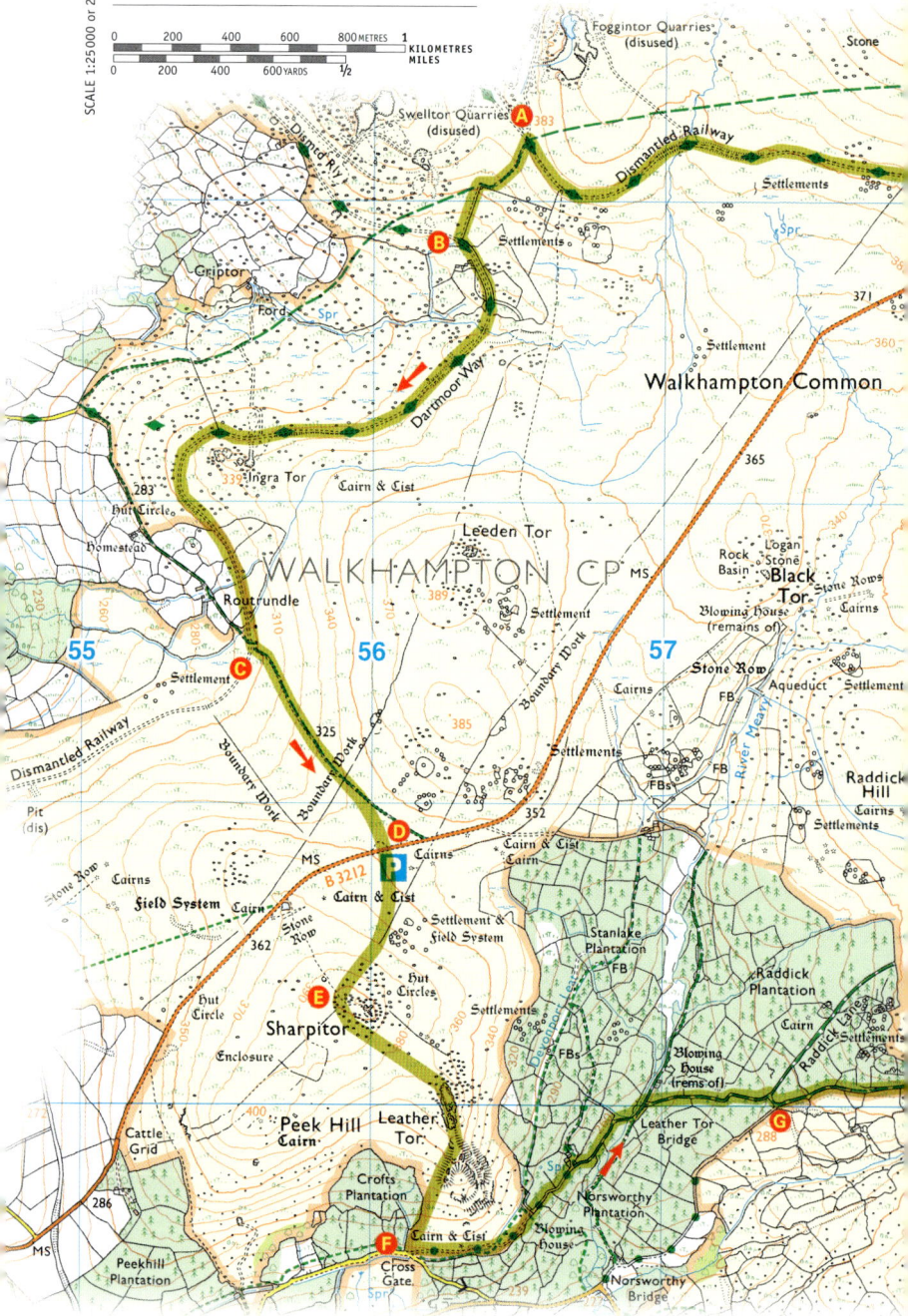

eventually to reach a gate. Go through the gate, continue gently downhill along a broad, walled track, go through another gate and keep ahead into Princetown, with **The Plume of Feathers** left and **Lord's Café** right.

walk 27

Dittisham, Cornworthy and Tuckenhay

Start
Dittisham

Distance
9½ miles (15.2km)

Height gain
1,790 feet (545m)

Approximate time
5½ hours

Route terrain
Undulating field and woodland paths, country lanes

P Parking
Dittisham Ham car park (pay & display) by River Dart

Dog friendly
On lead in farmland and through Cornworthy Court

OS maps
Landranger 202 (Torbay & South Dartmoor), Explorer OL20 (South Devon)

GPS waypoints
SX 864 550
A SX 853 550
B SX 846 551
C SX 831 553
D SX 829 555
E SX 832 564
F SX 818 560
G SX 816 551
H SX 824 551
J SX 836 544
K SX 851 545

This lengthy, varied and energetic route takes you through some of the finest inland scenery in the South Hams. It starts off beside a broad stretch of the River Dart, passes through three attractive and interesting villages, and also takes in farmland, woodland, meadowland and a lovely ramble alongside Bow Creek. This is hilly country and parts of the walk are quite strenuous with a number of steep 'ups and downs'. If the weather is wet there will be muddy tracks and during the summer it is quite likely that some of the field paths will become overgrown. From the higher parts of the walk the views are superb, in particular those overlooking the Dart.

Start by turning left at the car park toilet block along the right edge of the recreation area, by a hedge on the right. Bear right on to an enclosed, uphill path and at a T-junction turn right to continue uphill, negotiating a mixture of stiles, kissing-gates and steps, eventually bearing left up to a road. Turn right along it into Dittisham, a pleasant village of narrow lanes, old cottages and an impressive 14th- to 15th-century church in a fine position above the River Dart.

At a crossroads in the village centre keep ahead, in the Combe and Cornworthy direction, along a lane which bends left and heads downhill to continue beside Dittisham Mill Creek. Turn right A, at a public footpath sign, and cross the creek on a wooden footbridge to a tarmac track, under trees. Cross over and climb steps to a stile; turn left along a path which follows the contours across a sloping field above a stream. At the end of the field climb a stile and walk along an enclosed path (carpeted in wild garlic in spring) under trees, eventually passing through a gate onto a lane. Turn right B uphill through the hamlet of East Cornworthy, follow the lane round a left bend and continue steadily uphill. At the top there are grand views across the Dart to the village of Stoke Gabriel on the opposite side.

Descend to a crossroads, turn right C downhill along a narrow lane into the quiet and remote village of Cornworthy and at a junction turn right to pass attractive, mainly 15th-century, St Peter's Church. Almost immediately turn right

Dittisham Mill

D by the village hall and follow footpath signs through a farmyard (Cornworthy Court). Pass the farmhouse and turn right through two gates between farm buildings and continue downhill along an enclosed track. At the bottom follow a waymark to the left down a pleasant, tree- and hedge-lined track, later keeping along the right edge of a field to the shore of Bow Creek **E**, a delightful spot.

Turn left alongside the creek, climb a stile, walk along the foreshore and the path climbs above the creek. Continue, initially along an enclosed, tree-lined path below wooded slopes – a most attractive part of the walk – later along the bottom edge of a field. Keep alongside the creek; cross a meadow, then a footbridge, and the path continues into trees to a stile. Climb this, turn right at a footpath sign a few yards ahead to keep above the creek and follow the path up steps to a waymarked post. Bear right to continue along the bottom edge of a sloping field, and eventually follow the field

edge and creek left to a kissing-gate. Pass through and follow a narrow path through trees. Descend steps and later the path squeezes between a wire fence on the left and the trees bordering the creek on the right to reach a stone stile. Climb this and turn right over Tuckenhay Bridge to a T-junction.

Tuckenhay It is difficult to imagine that in Victorian times this peaceful village was a busy port with warehouses, paper mills, a corn mill, limekilns and a selection of other industrial enterprises. Tuckenhay was founded in 1806 by the ambitious Abraham Tucker, after whom it was named, but his grandiose plans were later ruined by the silting up of the harbour and nowadays the only reminders of its past activities are the two imposing paper mills at the top end of the village, which have been converted into private apartments.

At the T-junction turn left **F** along a lane, take the first turning on the left (Bridge Terrace), recross the stream and follow the lane to the right and uphill, passing the mill, which closed down in 1917. Continue along a track which heads steeply uphill through woodland and descends to a lane. Turn right, take the first turning on the left to walk along a tarmac track and, by a thatched cottage, turn left **G** along a track to a wooden gate. Go through, continue gently uphill along an enclosed track and pass to the left of barns to go through another wooden gate. Keep along the left edge of a sloping field, by a hedge on the left, as it curves right

uphill to a stile in the field corner. Climb this, keep ahead over a footbridge to climb another, pass a waymarked post and continue uphill, by a line of widely spaced trees on the left, to a waymarked post. Keep straight ahead up the left edge of the field and through a gate in the top corner to reach the lane at Furze Cross. Cross over and bear left along the lane signposted to Cornworthy, and at a public footpath sign turn right **H** on to a hedge-lined track.

Where the track turns sharp left bear right through a gate; bear left and head gently uphill along the left edge of a field. Go through a gate, continue along

SCALE 1:25 000 or 2½ INCHES to 1 MILE 4CM to 1KM

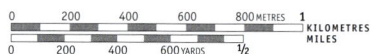

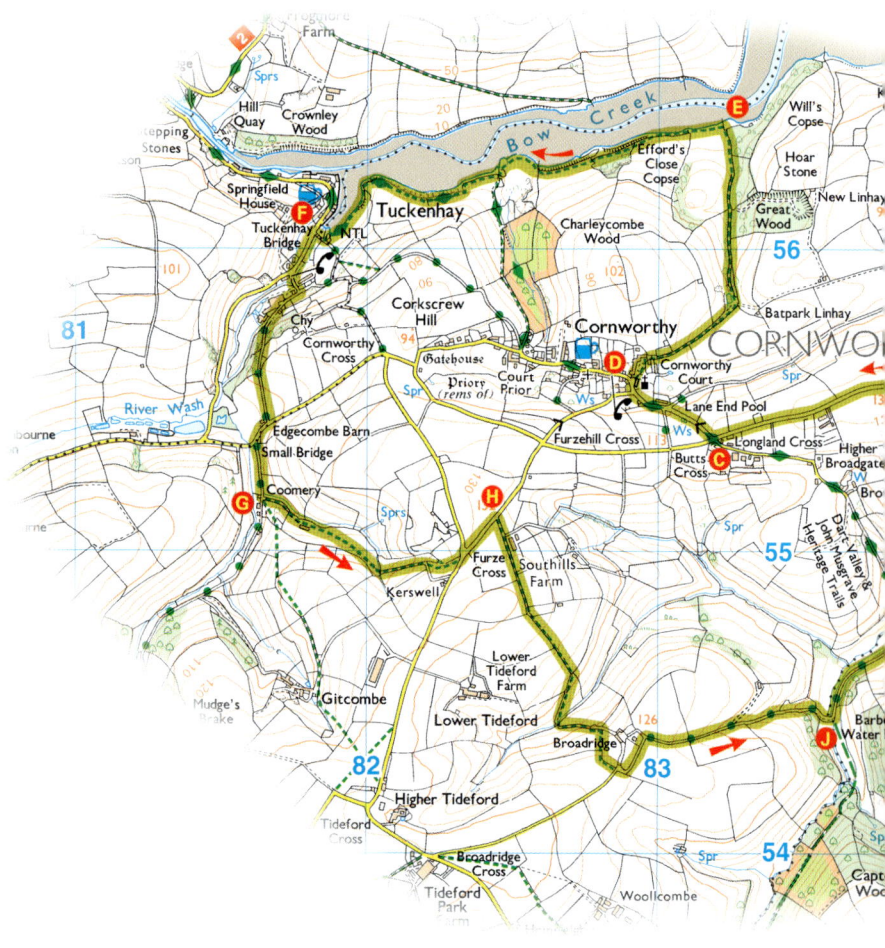

the left edge of the next field and go through another gate just before reaching the field corner. Keep along the right edge of the next field and descend steeply to pass through a gate. Follow the direction of a waymark diagonally downhill across a field and in the bottom corner bear left through a gate and over a footbridge. Bear right and almost immediately left and continue uphill along an enclosed path. At a waymarked post, bear right to continue uphill along the left edge of a field and follow the field edge to the right to pass through a gate. Keep along a fenced track with the hedge left and go through a metal gate onto a tarmac lane. Turn left along the lane, which bends left to reach the entrance to Broadridge House. Turn right along a rough, hedge-lined track, heading steeply downhill, and at the bottom cross a stream to another T-junction **J**.

Turn left along a tree-lined track which ascends gently, curving gradually right and later descends. Pass a path junction and keep ahead to a lane at Barberry Cross. Turn right along this narrow, winding and undulating lane. Follow it around a left bend and continue along it for ½ mile following signs for Dittisham, dropping steeply to where it bends left again. Just round the bend turn right **K** and go through a small gate to the right of a larger one at a public footpath sign. Turn left and cross the field diagonally, descending into a hollow then climbing to join the field edge at a corner by a public footpath sign. Follow the right edge of the field; as you proceed over the brow of the hill, a glorious view unfolds over the Dart valley, one of the finest on the walk.

Go through a gate and head gently downhill along the right edge of the next field to a kissing-gate and then continue down a shady, enclosed track to a lane. Turn right, here rejoining the outward route, into Dittisham and retrace your steps to return to the start.

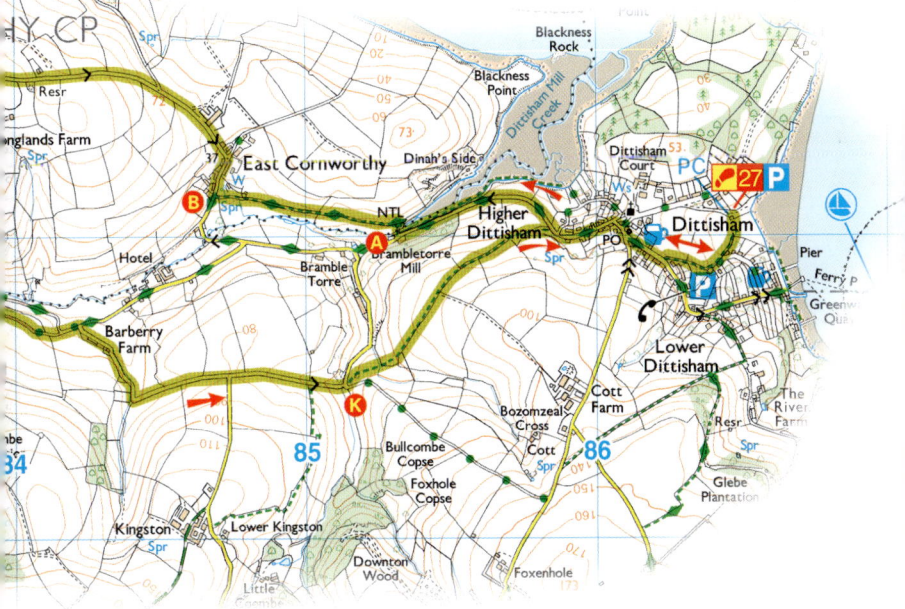

Buckfastleigh Moor

Start

Holne

Distance

10 miles (15.8km)

Height gain

1,855 feet (565m)

Approximate time

6 hours

Route terrain

Pathless moorland, some wet; steady ascent start to **C**; steep climb to finish

P Parking

Laneside in Holne near village hall

Dog friendly

Under control at all times; on lead in nesting season (1 March–15 July)

OS maps

Landranger 202 (Torbay & South Dartmoor), Explorer OL28 (Dartmoor)

GPS waypoints

 SX 706 694
A SX 702 688
B SX 696 689
C SX 668 698
D SX 659 690
E SX 672 673
F SX 685 659
G SX 700 666
H SX 702 674
J SX 710 681

At the beginning and end the route follows lanes and tracks, but the remainder of the walk is across the open – and in parts pathless – expanses of Buckfastleigh Moor. This is a long and quite demanding walk with a lot of rough going and boggy conditions can be expected after rain. On a fine day, however, this is a most invigorating walk with a great feeling of spaciousness and freedom, and offering superb and extensive views, especially along the crest of the low ridge from Ryder's Hill, over Snowdon and Pupers Hill to Water Oak Corner. Remember to leave some reserves of energy for the final, steep ½ mile pull back up to Holne.

⚠ Because much of it is across rather featureless moorland where the tracks are non-existent and landmarks are few, on no account should this route be attempted in misty conditions by inexperienced walkers; even those who are able to navigate using a compass may find the section between **C** and **D** difficult.

> **Holne** There is an off-the-beaten-track feel to Holne, tucked away amongst quiet side lanes, but its photogenic cottages, inn and medieval church make it one of the most charming of Dartmoor villages. The village also benefits from a community shop and tearoom.

 Turn left out of the car park along the lane. At a right-hand bend turn left again, in the Scoriton direction, and head downhill. The lane bends right and continues steeply down through the hamlet of Littlecombe to a left-hand bend **A**. Take the right lane, follow it for ¹/₂ mile into Michelcombe and, at another T-junction, turn left **B** along a lane signposted 'No Through Road, Bridleway Only'. Where the lane ends, keep ahead between gateposts, at a sign 'Bridlepath to the Moor', and continue steeply uphill along a sunken, enclosed, hedge-lined track which leads through a metal gate on to the open expanses of Buckfastleigh Moor.

Keep ahead along a wide, grassy track, faint but discernible, called the Sandy Way, passing to the right of the first tree that you see and continuing steadily uphill, soon crossing a stone footbridge over a leat and passing some stunted trees. Keep on in a north-westerly direction: from now on the views all around

Trees are a rarity on Buckfastleigh Moor

are superb. At a rough fork follow the more obvious track half-left (north-west), cutting a broad swathe through bracken, gorse and heather, soon heading in a more westerly direction.

Head up towards Holne Ridge, passing several stone posts with 'PUDC' inscribed on them. Pass to the left of an area of former tinworkings; Venford Reservoir can be seen in the distance below right. Towards the top of the ridge bear left **C** on a grassy track in a south-westerly direction and head across rough, grassy and often boggy moorland to Ryder's Hill. This can be difficult as there is no line of path and no obvious landmarks, apart from a worn track ahead that can be seen heading gently up to the top of the rise. After reaching this track, the vital landmark to make for is the triangulation pillar, and the standing stone beside it, on the 1,690-foot (515m) summit of Ryder's Hill **D**.

From now on route-finding becomes much easier. The next section is particularly exhilarating as you turn left and head in a south-easterly direction along the broad crest of the ridge, making for a cairn on the next

Petre's Bound Stone

The name of the standing stone on Ryder's Hill, indicates that it formerly marked the boundary of an estate. This is a magnificent vantage point over the empty moor, and in fine weather the view southwards extends across the South Hams to the coast.

hill, which though called Snowdon bears little resemblance to its more distinguished Welsh namesake. There is a discernible grassy track in places but conditions underfoot are likely to be soggy. From the cairn continue in the same direction along a gently undulating route, passing a second cairn about 100 yds farther on, to the rocks and cairn on Pupers Hill **E**, another grand viewpoint. Over to the left the tower of Buckfast Abbey is visible.

From here descend gradually on what is now a good, clear path, heading south-east and crossing a grassy track, the Two Moors Way, and soon Avon Dam Reservoir comes into view on the right. Finally the path bears left, towards Water Oak Corner, marked by a small, isolated group of trees dominated by a

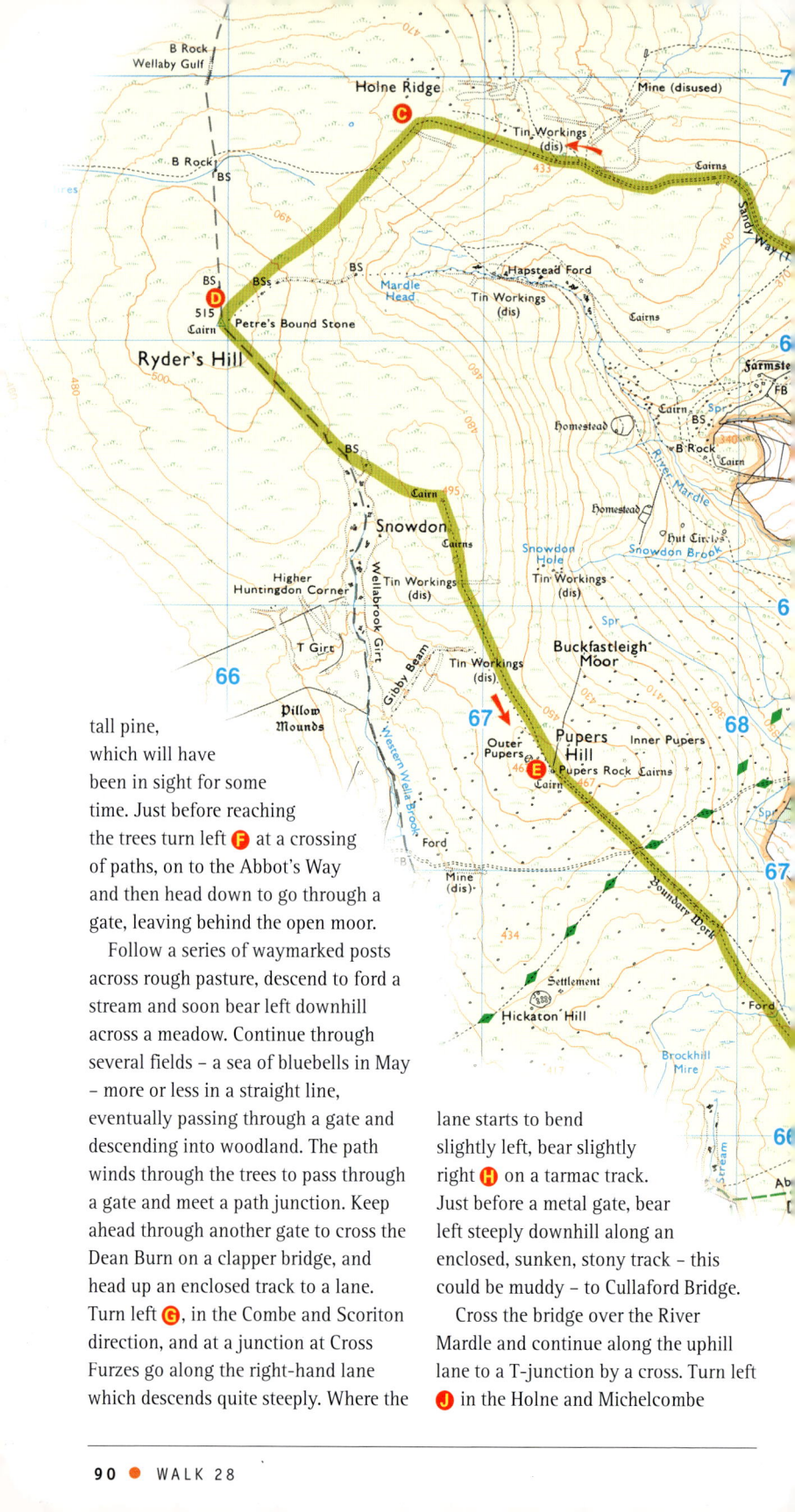

Map labels (top to bottom, left to right):
B Rock
Wellaby Gulf
Holne Ridge
C
Mine (disused)
Tin Workings (dis)
433
Cairns
B Rock
BS
Sandy Way (T
BS
BS
BSs
BS
Hapstead Ford
Tin Workings (dis)
Cairns
Marble Head
Farmste
FB
D
515
Cairn
Petre's Bound Stone
Ryder's Hill
500
480
BS
Cairn
Cairn
BS
B Rock
Cairn
River Mardle
Homestead
Homestead
Hut Circles
Snowdon
Cairns
Snowdon Hole
Snowdon Brook
Higher Huntingdon Corner
Tin Workings (dis)
Tin Workings (dis)
T Girt
Spr
66
Buckfastleigh Moor
Wellabrook Girt
Gibby Beam
Tin Workings (dis)
67
68
Dillow Mounds
Outer Pupers
Pupers Hill
Inner Pupers
E
Pupers Rock
Cairns
Cairn
Western Wella Brook
Ford
67
Mine (dis)
434
Boundary Work
Settlement
Hickaton Hill
Brockhill Mire
Stream
66
Ab

tall pine, which will have been in sight for some time. Just before reaching the trees turn left **F** at a crossing of paths, on to the Abbot's Way and then head down to go through a gate, leaving behind the open moor.

Follow a series of waymarked posts across rough pasture, descend to ford a stream and soon bear left downhill across a meadow. Continue through several fields – a sea of bluebells in May – more or less in a straight line, eventually passing through a gate and descending into woodland. The path winds through the trees to pass through a gate and meet a path junction. Keep ahead through another gate to cross the Dean Burn on a clapper bridge, and head up an enclosed track to a lane. Turn left **G**, in the Combe and Scoriton direction, and at a junction at Cross Furzes go along the right-hand lane which descends quite steeply. Where the lane starts to bend slightly left, bear slightly right **H** on a tarmac track. Just before a metal gate, bear left steeply downhill along an enclosed, sunken, stony track – this could be muddy – to Cullaford Bridge.

Cross the bridge over the River Mardle and continue along the uphill lane to a T-junction by a cross. Turn left **J** in the Holne and Michelcombe

direction. The lane descends and where it bends right at the bottom keep ahead at an 'Unsuitable for Motors' sign, along a steep, hedge-lined track for a final, tiring ½-mile climb. On joining a lane keep ahead into the village of Holne

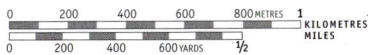

and well-earned refreshment at either the **Holne Tearoom** or **Church House Inn**.

SCALE 1:25000 or 2½ INCHES to 1 MILE 4CM to 1KM

Further Information

Safety on the Hills

The hills, mountains and moorlands of Britain, though of modest height compared with those in many other countries, need to be treated with respect. Friendly and inviting in good weather, they can quickly be transformed into wet, misty, windswept and potentially dangerous areas of wilderness in bad weather. Even on an outwardly fine and settled summer day, conditions can rapidly deteriorate at high altitudes and, in winter, even more so.

Therefore it is advisable always to take both warm and waterproof clothing, sufficient nourishing food, a hot drink, first-aid kit, torch and whistle. Wear suitable footwear, such as strong walking boots or shoes that give a good grip over rocky terrain and on slippery slopes. Try to obtain a local weather forecast and bear it in mind before you start. Do not be afraid to abandon your proposed route and return to your starting point in the event of a sudden and unexpected deterioration in the weather. Do not go alone and allow enough time to finish the walk well before nightfall.

Most of the walks described in this book do not venture into remote wilderness areas and will be safe to do, given due care and respect, at any time of year in all but the most unreasonable weather. Indeed, a crisp, fine winter day often provides perfect walking conditions, with firm ground underfoot and a clarity that is not possible to achieve in the other seasons of the year. A few walks, however, are suitable only for reasonably fit and experienced hill walkers able to use a compass and should definitely not be tackled by anyone else during the winter months or in bad weather, especially high winds and mist. These are indicated in the general description that precedes each of the walks.

Walkers and the Law

The Countryside and Rights of Way Act (CRoW Act 2000) extends the rights of access previously enjoyed by walkers in England and Wales. Implementation of these rights began on 19 September 2004. The Act amends existing legislation and for the first time provides access on foot to certain types of land – defined as mountain, moor, heath, down and registered common land.

Where You Can Go
Rights of Way
Prior to the introduction of the CRoW Act, walkers could only legally access the countryside along public rights of way. These are either 'footpaths' (for walkers only) or 'bridleways' (for walkers, riders on horseback and pedal cyclists). A third category called 'Byways open to all traffic' (BOATs), is used by motorised vehicles as well as those using non-mechanised transport. Mainly they are green lanes, farm and estate roads, although occasionally they will be found crossing mountainous area.

Rights of way are marked on Ordnance Survey maps. Look for the green broken lines on the Explorer maps, or the red dashed lines on Landranger maps.

The term 'right of way' means exactly what it says. It gives a right of passage over what, for the most part, is private land. Under pre-CRoW legislation walkers were required to keep to the line of the right of way and not stray onto land on either side. If you did inadvertently wander off the right of way, either because of faulty map reading or because the route was not clearly indicated on the ground, you were technically trespassing.

Local authorities have a legal obligation to ensure that rights of way are kept clear and free of obstruction, and are signposted where they leave metalled roads. The duty of local authorities to install signposts extends to the placing of signs along a path or way, but only where the authority considers it necessary to have a signpost or waymark to assist persons unfamiliar with the locality.

The New Access Rights
Access Land
As well as being able to walk on existing rights of way, under the new legislation you now have access to large areas of open land. You can of course continue to use rights of way footpaths to cross this land, but the main difference is that you can now lawfully leave the path and wander at will, but only in areas designated as access land.

Where to Walk
Areas now covered by the new access rights – Access Land – are shown on Ordnance Survey Explorer maps bearing the access land symbol on the front cover.

'Access Land' is shown on Ordnance Survey maps by a light yellow tint surrounded by a pale orange border. New orange coloured 'i' symbols on the maps will show the location of permanent access information boards installed by the access authorities.

Restrictions
The right to walk on access land may lawfully be restricted by landowners, but whatever restrictions are put into place on access land they have no effect on existing rights of way, and you can continue to walk on them.

Dogs
Dogs can be taken on access land, but must be kept on leads of two metres or less between 1 March and 31 July, and at all times where they are near livestock. In addition landowners may impose a ban on all dogs from fields where lambing takes place for up to six weeks in any year. Dogs may be banned from moorland used for grouse shooting and breeding for up to five years.

General Obstructions
Obstructions can sometimes cause a problem on a walk and the most common of these is where the path across a field has been ploughed over. It is legal for a farmer to plough up a path provided that it is restored within two weeks. This does not always happen and you are faced with the dilemma of following the line of the path, even if this means treading on crops, or walking round the edge of the field. Although the latter course of action seems the most sensible, it does mean that you would be trespassing.

Other obstructions can vary from overhanging vegetation to wire fences across the path, locked gates or even a cattle feeder on the path.

Use common sense. If you can get round the obstruction without causing damage, do so. Otherwise only remove as much of the obstruction as is necessary to secure passage.

If the right of way is blocked and cannot be followed, there is a long-standing view that in such circumstances there is a right to deviate, but this cannot wholly be relied on. Although it is accepted in law that highways (and that includes rights of way) are for the public service, and if the usual track is impassable, it is for the general good that people should be entitled to pass into another line. However, this should not be taken as indicating a right to deviate whenever a way is impassable. If in doubt, retreat.

Report obstructions to the local authority and/or the Ramblers.

Useful Organisations

Campaign for National Parks
Tel. 020 7924 4077
www.cnp.org.uk

Campaign to Protect Rural England
Tel. 020 7981 2800
www.cpre.org.uk

Dartmoor National Park Authority
Tel. 01626 832093
www.dartmoor-npa.gov.uk
Haytor Information Centre
Tel. 01364 661520
High Moorland Visitor Centre, Princetown
Tel. 01822 890414
Postbridge Information Centre
Tel. 01822 880272

English Heritage
Tel. 0870 333 1181
www.english-heritage.org.uk

Independent Hostels
Tel. 01629 580427
www.IndependentHostelsUK.co.uk

Long Distance Walkers' Association
www.ldwa.org.uk

National Trust
Devon Regional Office
Tel. 01392 881691
Membership and general enquiries
Tel. 0870 458 4000
www.nationaltrust.org.uk

Natural England
Tel. 0300 060 2481
www.naturalengland.org.uk

Ordnance Survey
Tel. 0845 05 05 05 (Lo-call)
www.ordnancesurvey.co.uk

Ramblers
Tel. 0207 339 8500
www.ramblers.org.uk

South West Coast Path Association
Tel. 01752 896237
www.swcp.org.uk

Youth Hostels Association
Tel. 0870 770 8868
www.yha.org.uk

Traveline: 0871 200 2233
www.traveline.org.uk
National train enquiry line:
08457 484950

Tourist information centres (South Devon)
Brixham: 01803 214885
www.torbay.gov.uk
Budleigh Salterton: 01395 445275
www.visitbudleigh.com
Dartmouth: 01803 834224
www.discoverdartmouth.com
Dawlish: 01626 621665
www.southdevon.org.uk
Exeter: 01392 265700
www.exeter.gov.uk
Exmouth: 01395 222299
www.exmouth-guide.co.uk
Honiton: 01404 43716
Newton Abbot: 01626 215667
www.teignbridge.co.uk
Ottery St Mary: 01404 813964
www.otterytourism.org.uk

Paignton: 0870 707 0010
www.torbay.gov.uk
Plymouth, Mayflower Centre:
01752 306330
www.plymouthcity.co.uk
Salcombe: 01548 843927
www.salcombeinformation.co.uk
Sidmouth: 01395 516441
www.visitsidmouth.co.uk
Teignmouth: 01626 215666
www.southdevon.org.uk
Torquay: 0870 707 0010
www.torbay.gov.uk
Totnes: 01803 863168
www.totnesinformation.co.uk
Tourist information centres (Dartmoor)
Okehampton: 01837 53020
www.okehamptondevon.co.uk
Tavistock: 01822 612938
www.tavistockonline.co.uk/tourist_info.htm
Community information centres (Dartmoor)
Ashburton: 01364 653426
www.ashburton.org
Bovey Tracey: 01626 832047
Buckfastleigh: 01364 644522
Ivybridge: 01752 897035
www.ivybridgewatermark.co.uk
Moretonhampstead: 01647 440043
www.moretonhampstead.com

Ordnance Survey maps of South Devon and Dartmoor

The walks described in this guide are covered by Ordnance Survey 1:50 000 scale (1¼ inches to 1 mile or 2cm to 1km) Landranger map sheets 191, 192, 201, 202. These all-purpose maps are packed with information to help you explore the area. Viewpoints, picnic sites, places of interest and caravan and camping sites are shown, as well as public rights of way information such as footpaths and bridleways.

To examine the area in more detail, and especially if you are planning walks, the Ordnance Survey Explorer maps at 1:25 000 scale (2½ inches to 1 mile or 4cm to 1km) are ideal. Maps covering the area are:
OL20 (South Devon)
OL28 (Dartmoor)
110 (Torquay & Dawlish)
114 (Exeter & the Exe Valley)
115 (Exmouth & Sidmouth)
116 (Lyme Regis & Bridport)

Acknowledgements
With grateful thanks to all those who keep me company during my ramblings (verbal
and otherwise), but in particular Brenda and Stuart.

Text: Brian Conduit and Sue Viccars
                   Revised text for 2012 edition, Sue Viccars
Photography: Brian Conduit and Sue Viccars.
                   Front cover: iStockphoto © Neil J
Editorial: Ark Creative (UK) Ltd
Design: Ark Creative (UK) Ltd

© Crimson Publishing 2012

Ordnance Survey®
Certified Partner

This product includes mapping data licensed from Ordnance
Survey® with the permission of the Controller of Her Majesty's
Stationery Office. © Crown Copyright 2012. All rights
reserved. Licence number 150002047. Ordnance Survey, the OS symbol and
Pathfinder are registered trademarks and Explorer, Landranger and Outdoor
Leisure are trademarks of the Ordnance Survey, the national mapping agency of
Great Britain.

ISBN: 978-1-78059-043-1

While every care has been taken to ensure the accuracy of the route directions, the
publishers cannot accept responsibility for errors or omissions, or for changes in
details given. The countryside is not static: hedges and fences can be removed,
stiles become gates, field boundaries can alter, footpaths can be rerouted and
changes in ownership can result in the closure or diversion of some concessionary
paths. Also, paths that are easy and pleasant for walking in fine conditions may
become slippery, muddy and difficult in wet weather, while stepping stones across
rivers and streams may become impassable.

   If you find an inaccuracy in either the text or maps, please write to Crimson
Publishing at the address below.

First published 1996 by Jarrold Publishing
Revised and reprinted 1998, 2003, 2005, 2006, 2007, 2009.

Printed in Singapore. 8/12

This edition first published in Great Britain 2012 by
Crimson Publishing,
Westminster House, Kew Road, Richmond, Surrey, TW9 2ND

www.crimsonpublishing.co.uk

All rights reserved. No part of this publication may be reproduced, transmitted in
any form or by any means, or stored in a retrieval system without either the prior
written permission of the publisher, or in the case of reprographic reproduction a
licence issued in accordance with the terms and licences issued by the CLA Ltd.

A catalogue record for this book is available from the British Library.

Front cover: Salcombe
Page 1: Green lane near Lower Whiddon

Unearth *The best of* Britain series
from Crimson Publishing

Accessible, contemporary guides by local experts

The best of Britain series includes...

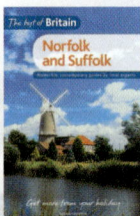

Norfolk and Suffolk

The Lake District

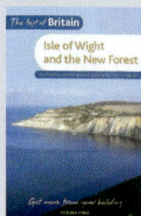

Isle of Wight and the New Forest

Northern Ireland

Devon

Cotswolds

Edinburgh and East Coast Scotland

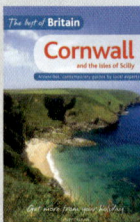

Cornwall and the Isles of Scilly

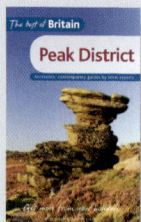

Peak District

Easy to navigate...informative and packed with practical information - *Which? Holiday*

crimson   www.crimsonpublishing.co.uk